The Extraordinary Truth about
Life on a Spanish Island

SANDWICHES
IN THE
Sun

by CHRIS HERMAN

iUniverse, Inc.
Bloomington

Sandwiches in the Sun
The Extraordinary Truth about Life on a Spanish Island

iUniverse books may be ordered through booksellers or by contacting:

iUniverse
1663 Liberty Drive
Bloomington, IN 47403
www.iuniverse.com
1-800-Authors (1-800-288-4677)

ISBN: 978-1-4759-6611-4 (sc)
ISBN: 978-1-4759-6610-7 (hc)
ISBN: 978-1-4759-6609-1 (e)

Library of Congress Control Number: 2012923067

Printed in the United States of America

iUniverse rev. date: 1/28/2013

I would like to take this opportunity to express my appreciation to all those who have helped to give us the possibility of moving to Lanzarote and fulfil our calling, and without whose continuing support, we would not be able to carry on.

Also to Si Jolly for his great pictures that you will find in the middle of this book. I really enjoyed our time together, touring the island and snapping up the sights.

Finally, and most importantly, I would like to thank my wife Sue for her support and encouragement, for all the work she put into reading, correcting and re-reading my manuscripts, for her endurance through the most difficult times in our life on Lanzarote, and above all for her unyielding devotion and love.

CONTENTS

CHAPTER 1

In the Beginning:
Life in a Canarian Finca

AT THE BEGINNING OF March 2006, we started our life in Lanzarote in Spain. We had only visited the island on a few brief occasions, so we started as guests of Mark and Julie Austin at Betel, a beautiful old—in parts dilapidated—*finca,* or farmhouse, standing quietly on a high plane of lava at the epicentre of this volcanic island.

Its thick stone walls were built to keep out the blistering midday heat of the sun, which beats relentlessly down with the same strength as it does on the sandy wastes of the African continent, less than a day's flight to the east for the flocks of swallows that occasionally arrive here, blown off their yearly northward course toward our erstwhile home back in the United Kingdom. By day the harsh brightness of the sun bounces off the pristinely whitewashed walls, while at night the pitch-black sky spreads above it like a giant vacuous dome, sprinkled with myriads of sparkling pinpricks that multiply by the million as the human eye accustoms itself to the clear, deep darkness, untouched by the pollution of light from streetlamps.

We had arrived just in time for warm spring days that average twenty-four degrees Celsius right until the coming of summer in July. The warmth of the Lanzarote welcome was completed by our generous and genial hosts, who also complement one another superbly. Julie's quiet spirituality draws like a brightly flickering candle, while Mark effuses enthusiasm and boisterous banter. While Julie conjured up the most aromatic and succulent cooking, only Mark had the strength and skill to crank up the cantankerous old diesel-powered generator, which was the main source of the house's electricity.

Within the ancient walls of our temporary new residence, you could say we enjoyed all the modern conveniences, but not always in the desired quantity. On an average day there was usually enough electricity to power one load in the washing machine. We had water on tap as long as there was power to run the pump, and piping hot water would run as long as the temperamental gas cylinder allowed.

There was even 'central heating'! Central heating? Was that really necessary? Well, those thick stone walls that maintained a comfortable coolness during the peak of the summer turned the place into a fridge once the sun had gone down outside during the hottest months. The 'central' heating came courtesy of a freestanding gas fire, parked hopefully in the centre of the cavernous thirty-by-twenty-foot living room, or 'chapel', with its crumbling lofty ceiling, and whose supply would splutter disappointingly to exhaustion at all-too-frequent intervals.

In fact, I can honestly say I've never been so cold in my life before. I remember vividly, and with a shiver, the nights the heater failed. At first we would augment our jumpers and coats with a blanket, fetched hurriedly from our bedroom on the opposite side of the courtyard.

Soon we'd return for a second, and not long after that we'd be wrapped up in bed. There was just nowhere else to go to escape the bitter, penetrating chill.

Despite its basic drawbacks, we still remember the old place with fondness. Along with the peace and quiet of its location, there was the beauty of the architecture, so typically Canarian, with carefully crafted black volcanic stone blocks picked out against the smooth white walls, the sprawling, feathery canopy of the pepper tree half filling the space where we parked our cars outside the solid rustic wooden front door, together with the bright red flowers and pea-green foliage of the crown of thorns shrubs that ran the length of the low white retaining wall, which separated the parking from the 'garden'.

The 'garden' was a small area of plants sitting proudly on a bed of *picón*, the black volcanic grit that's used everywhere here as a gravelly mulch to help retain the heavy dews upon which the local plant life relies. Beyond that stood a long row of netted, wood-framed housing, which reminded me of the constructions my dad used to grow gooseberries in when I was a child. However, the inhabitants of these particular constructions were good for neither a crumble pudding nor a vegetarian supper. Neither were they good for our sleep, because living no more than forty feet from the shutters and ironwork that constituted our creaky bedroom windows was a den of fighting cockerels that you could set your alarm clock by—that is, if you were a baker and wanted to rise early every morning, several hours before the sun had even thought of rising.

Although the barbaric practice of bullfighting has long been outlawed in the Canaries, the 'sport' of pitching one pugnacious cockerel against another is still *en vigor*, as they say here, still vigorously pursued. And one of its proudest proponents was the ageing, shambling, but still tall and strong, landlord of Betel, Don Arturo.

He was a loveable old rogue really, our *dueño*. Always friendly with a gentle smile and a gruff chuckle, his customary reply to the Spanish greeting, *'Hola, Don Arturo, ¿cómo estás?'* was that he was struggling on in the *batalla de la vida*—the battle of life, as he called it. I wonder if that was a subliminal reference to his battling livestock.

The only time he reprimanded me, he was straightforward and not in the least disrespectful. The problem was, since Betel was situated bang in the middle of nowhere, access by motorised vehicle was, to put it bluntly, extremely bumpy. The unmade 'driveway' had somehow become rutted into a regular pattern, reminiscent of the rivulets that form in the sand on Bournemouth beach when the tide recedes. My mind wanders back to those warm afternoons in the late summer and the knobbly feeling underfoot as I used to paddle along the seashore over the compact sodden mass of sand.

In order to reduce the cacophony of rattling bones, chassis, and exhaust and cut down the anxiety that any of these might disintegrate at any moment, the driver had two options: take it really, really slowly or get up some steam and try to skim over the top of the bone-shaking bumps. I usually took the first option, counselling myself philosophically that it was a simple reminder of the general slow pace of life in Lanzarote. However, one day, when time was unusually pressing, I boldly went for the speedy approach. Unfortunately, the dry, dusty hardness of Lanzarote dirt tracks contrasts markedly with the damp, forgiving nature of Bournemouth sand. Accordingly I arrived with extraordinary rapidity at the gateway of Betel and was startled to see Don Arturo, consternated but still calm. As I complied with his simple request to turn round and behold the cloud of dust that accompanied my trail, it was enough to shame me into future obedience to the request to take it more gently.

Toward the end of our stay, Mark and Julie had an appliance fitted that made all the difference to their living quarters on the first floor of the southern wing: a wood-burning stove! Wood is in short supply here since the cedar forests that once covered the island were all used up about five hundred years ago to build fine houses and sturdy boats.

Nevertheless, Mark's son, Ben, being a carpenter, they were blessed with a sufficient supply of off-cuts to feed the nightly flames.

Our hosts being ever open and welcoming, we never felt we were intruding when we would sneak upstairs to find refuge in their cosy living room with their sleeping quarters off to the right and those of their four-year-old daughter, Naomi, off to the left. On occasion we'd be invited up for a special evening revolving around a nice bottle of red wine and a DVD chosen carefully from the nearest hire place, a ten-minute drive through the bumpy lava fields and into the local town of San Bartolomé, with its narrow streets and quaint shops masquerading as ordinary Lanzarote homes behind their whitewashed walls and plain green doors and shutters.

We always had fun on those evenings together, comparing amusing notes about life on the island and in the church. Somehow, though, the choice of DVD was always a bit unconventional. I remember one particular offering that reminded me of some of the French films we'd watched back in England. Of these, the one that has stayed with me above all was where the story came to a sudden end with the main character turning up unexpectedly at the home of the family to whose children she'd been the nanny, and gunning them all down, leaving the impression that the makers were either trying to make some rather dark philosophical point or had abruptly run out of budget.

But back to Betel and a cosy evening with the lights down low sitting around the wood burner in front of the flickering TV screen. It was a 'blockbuster' starring the great comic actor Bill Murray, whose performances we had relished over and again in films such as *Groundhog Day*. It turned out that this role was meant to be rather more serious, and with it, somewhat more strange. As the whole bizarre plot unfolded, I was tickled constantly by the ridiculous script and random sequence of events with the result that the rest of the company confessed to finding the general delirium engendered by my series of hysterical outbursts the real entertainment of the evening.

Our stay at Betel was a difficult time for my wife Sue, as she was experiencing a feeling of total helplessness. She had left her home and job behind and found herself unable to speak the language or even drive anywhere. Her sadness came to a head one day. Mark and Julie noticed that Sue was not her usual bubbly self. The simple inquiry, 'Are you okay?' opened the floodgates. We quickly ascended the stone stairway to their comfy sitting room, as they brought Sue consolation, talking sympathetically through her distraught emotions.

But the oddest occurrence in the short history of our occupation of the remote *finca* was reserved for the final weeks, when Mark had taken his family on holiday to France and left us in charge. This was the stimulus for us to move out for the week and enjoy a break on the sunny south side of the island that would later become our home. About halfway through the period, a report reached us that Bella the rabbit, the family's one and only pet and furry focus of little Naomi's affection, had been found dead as the result of a single mysterious and bloody bite to the back of the neck. Thankfully it was Ben who had found the poor creature and duly disposed of its lifeless form. But the problem remained, how would we explain this to its unfortunate owners?

As we returned to resume our residence, the series of strange events turned even more bizarre. We were greeted by the phlegmatic Don Arturo with a new example of the local wildlife in tow: a very sweet-looking kitten that danced around in a manner reminiscent of the young Cassius Clay. 'I don't know, but it looks like it could do with some food to me', was Arturo's comment as he foisted the kitten upon us. Thus, Bella the rabbit was replaced by the new little scrap of life. In the words of the Old Testament character Job, the most extreme example of changing fortunes, 'The Lord gives, and the Lord takes away'.

CHAPTER 2

Leaving the Stress Behind

ACTUALLY, LIFE WASN'T THAT bad in sometimes-sunny Bournemouth, my place of work for twenty-three years. I had just two jobs in that time, one long and happy marriage, and a brace of delightful children: a strapping son and a beautiful daughter. So we were well settled and privileged to enjoy the sort of stable family life that most people these days can only dream of.

There was really only one fly in the ointment of my life: work stress, and I mean with a capital S. Not that the two companies I had the variable pleasure of working for were bad employers—on the contrary, the first one, Abbey Life, had given me an excellent grounding in my chosen career of computer programming. They looked after their employees well and the location— a five-minute lunchtime jog from the long golden beaches that stretch from the Purbecks in the west all the way to Hengistbury Head in the east—was unbeatable.

My second job was more high-powered. I stepped up into the dizzy world of international finance in December 1989 when I climbed onboard with Chase Manhattan bank a few weeks before the start of the mildest winter in three centuries.

Its Bournemouth offices, situated in several acres of parkland on the eastern edge of the town, boasted all sorts of fantastic facilities for the benefit of its staff: tennis courts, squash courts, a well-equipped gym, a sports hall, a wonderful subsidised restaurant, as well as access to the public sports centre five minutes across the park.

I worked with characters much like me, who enjoyed working with figures, supported one another, and were essentially just pleasant to spend the working day with. I soon found my niche writing complicated mathematical programs for the bank's huge number-crunching machines.

Toward the end of 1994 I was working really hard to complete a particular project. It involved writing a number of new programs to produce figures for the bank's credit monitoring system. They had to be ready in just one week, so I applied myself with my customary enthusiasm, staying late every night. I remember the Friday especially well. We had invited some new friends, Steve and Jane from church, to dinner. I finally got home just in time to bid our guests good-night. I was so embarrassed!

The effect of bashing away at the keyboard relentlessly for so many hours was the beginning of aches and pains in my fingers and wrists. Being desperate to complete the task at hand, I kept going in spite of it. The pain naturally grew worse until finally I was forced to go sick. My initial week of absence turned into three months.

That time was spent seeing specialists and receiving physiotherapy. I went back to work eventually, mornings only to start with. It didn't help that my boss didn't have a sympathetic bone in his body. When

I told him how it was a bit frustrating having only half a day to make progress on my current project, he could only ask why I didn't stay longer! I was now working with my wrists supported in metal splints, thus partly reducing the constant pain that was like somebody sticking a needle into them and manipulating it to produce the maximum discomfort possible.

I struggled on for eight difficult years. Exercising in the gym provided by the company helped my hands, and I managed to go without using splints; but the pain persisted. On the positive side, I was privileged to have some very good support from a rheumatologist, and I remember telling him once how the answer to my prayers would be redundancy. Only that would afford me the opportunity to escape my stressful working environment and retrain to do something completely different.

I could hardly dare hope that my dream would come true. Then at ten o'clock one morning late in June 2002, I was sitting at my desk when I received a phone call from my boss, asking me to come upstairs to see him in the conference room. I knew immediately what was happening; the recent merger between the bank and JP Morgan meant there would be redundancies in banking positions.

I bounded up the stairs and burst through the door wearing a huge grin from ear to ear. Now, I am known for having an unusually wide smile, but on this occasion it must have been an unbelievable sight. Toby was sitting quietly on the other side of a conference table, a smartly dressed girl from human resources next to him. They talked sombrely and in hushed tones about their regret at having to let me go. I tried to dispel their gloomy air and explain that I was delighted, as if they could not already see that from my extraordinary appearance. I failed miserably. I guess it would be hard for anybody to take on board the fact that an employee should receive such bad news so gladly.

The company gave us lots of help in order to determine what direction our careers would now take. There were all sorts of psychometric tests, interviews with experts, and so on. However, I felt I needed to go further. I'd had a sneaking suspicion for some little while that I might be dyslexic. Could this be the reason I had always struggled in my chosen career of computer programming? Sure enough, the test revealed that whereas my verbal intelligence was high enough, there was a big gap between that and my brain's processing speed. Furthermore, the results showed poor eye-to-hand coordination, which explains why I was always so slow working at the screen and keyboard. Having dyslexia had also made it difficult to retain all the detailed technical information I needed to do my job properly. It was amazing I had stuck with it so long!

*   *   *   *   *

As I explored the different options, there was one I hardly dared to consider. Since the beginning of my career in computers, I'd had a hankering to go to Bible college to study theology. The desire had never been so strong that it had overcome the reluctance to return to academic application, which I had always found hard going. Now, though, as I considered what I really would like to do with the rest of my working life, that option became more and more attractive, and I soon signed up for the first year of study. Thankfully there was a tutor there who was very good at helping dyslexic students like myself. I thought that probably after a year of study and practical training I would discover my real vocation.

In the event, one year wasn't enough. I really benefited from the study and practice, but I still hadn't found my calling. Thankfully, Sue had been promoted from secretary to the manager of burials at a Woodland Burial Ground, to the manager's position itself, which meant we could afford for me to continue the degree course. A year turned into two and two became three, and I finally graduated with a degree, as well as discovering my calling to serve as assistant pastor in the English-speaking Family Church in Lanzarote.

Toward the end of the second year at college, we were to be sent away for ten days in teams to help local churches in special activities, such as holiday clubs for children, festivals, and other ways of reaching out to the community. I was to be dispatched with a team of nine, including my personal tutor, Martin, to help the Family Church in Puerto del Carmen put on a weeklong Festival for the Family. To my horror, I was even given the leadership of the team. *It must be because I speak Spanish,* I thought.

In order to prepare the way, Sue and I took advantage of a last-minute-bargain long weekend a month before the festival was due to start. As we planned our trip, the terrible news of the March 11 Madrid train bombings was hitting the headlines. The country was convulsing with distress, while the attacks changed the course of Spanish history, with the socialists winning the national elections three days later.

It felt like a historic time as we touched down mid-afternoon on the first of April. A recent shower had left the tarmac damp underfoot, and as we made our way across to the terminal, we looked up to see the most beautiful rainbow. It gave Sue a sense of hope and promise, which was so important. If we were going to leave our life in England behind, it would be more difficult for her than me.

Having elected 'allocation on arrival', we found ourselves lapping up the luxury of a spacious apartment on a beautifully quiet complex at the back of Costa Teguise. As we strolled along, Sue found the beauty of the white buildings, green palms, and deep-blue sky absolutely captivating. It was a good start, as the phantom of a grubby black rock, nicknamed 'Lanza-grotty' was dispelled from her mind.

Our first meal was the happy result of a reliable recommendation from the helpful receptionist, Nick. It was within walking distance, and we enjoyed the thirty-minute promenade through the palm tree-lined residential streets to the atmospheric accompaniment of cicadas rasping their evening song. The restaurant, La Jordana, turned out to be a very smart establishment. It had even been frequented by King Juan Carlos himself while his mother was still alive and residing in Las Maretas, one of his most distinguished holiday palaces that occupies a big chunk of coast a stone's throw away. Here we discovered the delights of sea bass and its pleasant partnership on the palate with the semisweet white wine, San Valentín. Combined with the splendid surroundings and impeccable service, it made for a thoroughly memorable outing.

The next morning we jumped onto a bus and took the one-hour journey to the old town of Puerto del Carmen. We found the church in a shopping centre, where Mark, who was pastor, had converted one of the units into a beautiful chapel. We also found a warm welcome from the residents of English-speaking origin, who formed the regular congregation. After the morning service, we spent time with Mark and his wife, Julie, and looked at the site for the festival.

The resulting event, a month later, was hard work, as we rose early each morning to make our preparations, and set up the stage and the stalls every afternoon. By the time we had finished for the day, had some food, and got ready for bed, it was well past midnight. It was a huge challenge for us, working alongside the small church, to run events in such a public place, with hundreds of people passing by. Our team took responsibility for the children's activities that included face painting and storytelling. Simply erecting the gazebo that provided shelter from the fierce African sun was a job and a half in itself, as six of us struggled against the wind.

One of the hardest things as leader was managing one of the young men. His unrequited attraction to one of the girls was proving to be a complete distraction for him. Not only that, it was disrupting our work as he pursued the girl in question with others of us trying to restrain him, while the object of his passion was really upset and surrounded by the other girls. It was a steep learning curve. On top of all that, we found that the square we were using had been double-booked most days. The first party to share the space with us put up a large tent, offering locally produced food and drinks. After an initial confrontation, they proved to be reasonably accommodating, and their presence drew yet more people to our own activities.

The next group to challenge our occupancy turned up early on the Wednesday evening and proved rather less easy to share the space with. The first thing that alerted us to their arrival was the distinctive rumble of gutsy motorcycle engines. Within a matter of minutes the harbour side of the square was filling up with leather-clad bikers, an array of impressive machines, and a good number of spectators. I was reluctant to give up our activities with the children, but it became clear very quickly that it was unsafe to continue.

Mark was quick to act. Finding an officer from the local police, he protested, 'You can't allow this. It's dangerous; there are small children here!'

'And where is your permit?' demanded the officer.

Mark showed him the official paper, duly signed and stamped.

'Well, their permit is obviously better than yours', the officer dismissively concluded.

Mark's astonishment was only equalled by our joint sense of frustration. We quickly got to packing up our stands and shepherding our young charges to safety. We were now at the pinnacle of what was proving to be a testing experience. I was so grateful for the presence of my tutor at this point.

With the motorcycle engines roaring in the background, he turned to me and shouted, 'Well, Chris, this is where you can be thankful …'

I wondered what Martin had found in the midst of all this difficulty that I could be thankful for.

'… that you've been blessed with a future focused temperament. You can see past the present difficulties'.

Martin's comment helped me to regain a positive attitude. Having abandoned our plans for the rest of the evening, we relaxed and began to enjoy the scene unfolding before us. It turned out to be highly entertaining, as a host of different machines from shiny black vintage Harley-Davidsons to rugged yellow dirt bikes gathered in rows, their riders engaged in a series of antics.

The slow bike race cracked the most smiles, as a grinning, toothless old hippy showed off his superior balance and stayed well behind his two competitors. The most breath-taking stunt then followed. The feat started with two muscular men sitting astride two very solid-looking Honda Gold Wings. As they circled slowly, six more of the most daring individuals clambered on top of them, one by one, until a human pyramid was teetering around the square and the whole ensemble had us all transfixed in a mixture of fear and wonderment.

'*Wahnsinn!*' ('Crazy!') the man next to me said.

I had spotted him standing on his own watching as the race was finishing, and I placed myself quietly at his side, hoping for an opportunity to air my rusty old German language skills. '*Irre!*' I agreed in German with the sentiment. '*Wissen Sie hier was los ist?*' ('Do you know what's going on here?') I asked.

'It's our annual gathering. Those guys are crazy; somebody's going to break their neck one day!'

As we got to chatting, he gave me his take on life on the island, and we exchanged opinions and information about our respective events.

'Are there many Germans living on the island then?' I asked.

'Quite a few. They're mostly on the run from the law!'

'Really?'

He explained how Lanzarote was still a haven for people evading prosecution for a whole host of misdemeanours perpetrated in their homeland.

As he turned to go, I caught the eye of a blonde woman in her thirties, spectating with two other ladies.

'*Schönen Spektakl, nicht wahr?*' ('Quite a sight, isn't it?') I ventured.

'Yes. What's going on? Are you with the bikers?'

'No. I'm with the Festival for the Family'.

As she and her two companions quizzed me further, the conversation quickly deepened. I was struck by how much more ready these people were to debate religious topics than the other nationalities I'd encountered during the week. Our well-laid plans had been disrupted again, but at least I was coming away refreshed by their openness and encouraged that my rusty German had been effective.

A Spanish-speaking voice was the next to interrupt my thoughts. It was Hugo, the Colombian pastor from Playa Blanca. 'Chris, we're going under the stage to pray. Come on'.

I followed him to the door behind the stage and down the steps into the gloomy storeroom. Half a dozen or so of our fellow church leaders were already gathered. As the others raised their voices and shouted their prayers, I was a bit taken aback.

I joined in rather more quietly. 'Lord, thank you that you're not deaf to our prayers!'

Ten minutes later we emerged into the warm early evening sunshine and immediately noticed a change. The crowd was already dispersing, as a steady stream of motorcyclists was burbling noisily up the hill away from the harbour. Straightaway we set about preparing for our evening programme. The young people from Hugo's church danced and sang first. It was a colourful spectacle, and we couldn't help singing and dancing along as they beat out their catchy Latin rhythms.

The climax of the evening was to be an address by a compelling gospel preacher from Tenerife. As he took to the stage and proclaimed the good news that people could start a new life by acknowledging the claims of Jesus Christ, he demonstrated the power of God in a spectacular and surprising healing.

Tracey from the Family Church had gone up to ask him to pray for her husband, Phil. As he began to speak out his prayer, the preacher gently placed one hand on her back. Tracey had not told him anything about the pain she had been experiencing in that area, or the way it had been steadily restricting her movements more and more over a period of months. Suddenly she felt a surge of power run through her body like electricity. The next moment she was running backward and forward the length of the square, excitedly shouting, 'I've been healed! I've been healed!'

What an amazing climax to the day's activities!

The fun continued as we retired to the Crafty Cow, one of the multitude of Irish bars along the coastal strip in Puerto del Carmen. A prominent member of the church, Patrick, was performing his Rolf Harris tribute. It turned out to be highly entertaining and very worthy of the well-loved Antipodean. Having finally climbed into bed a little after one a.m., I lay buzzing with the day's events. The only thing I could do with my excited thoughts was to turn them into prayer: 'Wow! That was awesome, Lord …' I continued like that for some time.

It was an intense time for Mark as pastor as well. As we combined our efforts and complemented each other, he concluded, 'You know, we make a great team, you and I. We really bring out the best in one another'. He had already asked me to consider coming back on a permanent basis in order to be his assistant pastor.

Returning to my studies, I reflected on the hurly-burly of those ten days, already convinced that Lanzarote was to be my destination. As I consulted Martin, my pastors, and the church where Sue and I had been members since its founding twenty years previously, everyone agreed. Nevertheless, Sue understandably had to be convinced that the calling was unequivocally from God. She had to hear for herself.

Nine months later I was back for six weeks to investigate the serious possibility of taking up residence on the island.

As I shadowed Mark and was introduced to the different personalities in the church, he explained to me the extraordinary character of British expats. They were all larger-than-life, but perhaps the greatest example was Paula. As we drove to see her in her little flat under the flight path of the planeloads of tourists taking off from Lanzarote airport, Mark gave me some background. With her bold character and broad northern accent, Paula had been employing her sense of humour in a unique singing and comedy act, for which she was well known and loved by locals and tourists alike. Then suddenly, three years ago, she had contracted an exceptionally aggressive type of cancer called non-Hodgkin's lymphoma and been given just a few months to live. As the church prayed and the Canarian doctors applied the chemotherapy, she would fly to Gran Canaria for her treatment each week and then be back at work for the weekend.

'The other patients would ask me what I was doing there. I was laughing and joking, while they hardly had the strength to sit up in bed!' she commented as she related the story to me. Having lost her hair, she even incorporated her baldness into her comic routine. 'I would wait until the end of the night and ask if anyone ever felt like tearing their hair out and then I would chuck my wig at folk. This would throw them as they couldn't work out if I was a man in drag or what!' Although Paula had been in remission for some time, she was starting to experience some worrying signs that the disease may be rearing its ugly head once more.

Another lively character, although not a member of the church, was Phil. My first memory of Phil is sitting on a hotel terrace in twenty-one degrees of January sunshine, slowly sipping a shandy, and chewing the fat with him and Mark after an energetic round of squash. Being a man of few words myself, I was able to sit back and take in the beautiful surroundings while Mark and he engaged in their typically animated conversation about the current lamentable state of the local sign-writing business, in which they were both engaged.

As the discussion turned to the weather, I was rather disappointed to learn from Phil that the formerly lovely climate had changed abruptly and radically in the two years prior. I took it as being on good authority that the winters had become wet, cloudy, and cool where before they were reliably dry, sunny, and warm. The evidence was there before our eyes even; the countryside had taken on a decidedly green tinge, with the sprouting into life of all sorts of grasses and wild plants. I put it down to the global phenomenon of climate change. *I guess the islands must be particularly susceptible to it,* I thought. Oh well, we hadn't come here for the weather, but to follow our vocation. So, although this was bad news, in the end it would be of no consequence.

Mark was just starting an informal squash club. He was a master of the game, and Phil not only matched his skill but was also physically well built. His cropped hair and tank-like form gave him the appearance of a kind of Rambo-like Vietnamese war veteran as he strode around the court with unrelenting strength and vigour. For me it was a chance to revive my interest in the sport and be given a good run-around. In time we were joined by other men like us, who, not content with the ambient warmth of our surroundings, preferred to throw ourselves around a hot, airless little room for an hour or so in pursuit of an annoyingly fast little black rubber ball in order to lose two litres of bodily fluid, so we had a good excuse to sit down and replace it with a delightfully refreshing mixture of cold Canarian Dorada beer and Sprite lemonade.

A fortnight into the visit, the pain of being separated from my beloved for the longest time in our twenty-five years of marriage was thankfully interrupted by a two-week visit from her. For a week of those two, we were able to move out of the cold old finca, where I had been staying with Mark and Julie, and take up temporary residence in a spacious, warm, and sunny holiday flat in Costa Teguise. The Monday of the week happened to be Sue's birthday. The day was hers to choose how to spend, and she naturally selected shopping as the morning activity.

Accordingly, once we got going for the day, we set out to find the commercial heart of Arrecife. This turned out to be no mean task.

Having spent some time going round in circles and queuing in the traffic that filled the narrow streets, we eventually found a parking space. As I began to carefully manoeuvre the Citroen hire car into the chosen slot and pulled the gear lever into the reverse position, the whole thing, knob and stick together, came out of its place. I was now stranded, with the front of the car protruding obstructively into the street and unable to drive forward. Not the best way to start a shopping outing, which I only tolerate even at the best of times! Thankfully, the object slotted back into place just as easily as it had come out. The episode behind us, we set off to explore the local stores.

The problem was that it was now nearly one o'clock. You guessed it! A few minutes after our arrival, everything was shut down for siesta; the place was deserted and would remain so until five. To add to poor Sue's sadness, it then started raining!

Sue's miserable birthday was thankfully redeemed by our favourite recreational activity: eating out in a fabulous restaurant that we could afford with our then valuable and plentiful pounds, which were able to stretch comfortably to the hundred euro bill—something we've not been in a position to repeat since!

Sue had been devouring the popular *Living in Spain*-type magazines ever since our first visit. Featuring in a prominent double page spread in the latest edition, complete with an inviting photograph of the happy couple walking along a wide, golden, deserted beach, were the new owners of an intriguing little restaurant. The latter was located conveniently and snugly behind the typically Canarian, plain, whitewashed chapel in Macher, a short ride from where we were staying. Having had our appetites whetted by the glowing report, we walked into a simple interior set with just six tables, or twenty-four covers, as our chef friend, Paul, would later term it.

We were served by the lady of the house, Debbie. My immediate impression was of an elegant, pretty, and professional hostess, her friendly welcome complementing the intimacy of the setting. When we mentioned the magazine, we were surprised to find that, although she obviously remembered the interview and photo call, Debbie had no idea that anything had actually gone to print. An interesting and compelling conversation opened up as we told her how we were about to follow in her footsteps, and she in turn related her experience of living and working on the island that we were considering making our home. It was a pity that her husband, Darren, who normally ran the kitchen, was unwell and unable to add his touch to either the meal or the story.

As we returned home, I finished my last few assignments and spent some time shadowing our friend Clive, who was senior pastor at the Christchurch Baptist Church. My placement finished there shortly before the end of the final term of study. As the three of us sat together in Clive's office, sipping coffee and reflecting on our changing circumstances, Clive turned to Sue.

'You won't believe this now, but you're going to really miss your job when you move to Lanzarote'.

'How do you mean?' she enquired.

'Well, you've had a lot of responsibility, and I've seen you revelling in that. You'll suddenly be without all that. It'll be a proper bereavement. I just think you need to be prepared for that', he explained.

Little did he know!

With my studies finished and my graduation behind us, we turned our minds to getting things in order for our new life in Lanzarote. Astonishingly, we sold our home within two weeks of placing it on the market, and by December 2005 we were making our final preparations to leave England. At the same time, our daughter, Ali, was getting ready for a Christmas wedding, while our son, Jonna, was about to leave for a six-month stint working for a charity in Bolivia.

Originally, Ali had wanted to tie the knot on Christmas Eve but was soon persuaded that the day before would be rather more convenient for the one hundred guests she was planning to invite!

In fact, it turned out to be perfect timing for a number of practical reasons. For us personally, it meant the satisfaction of seeing our only daughter happily married, while allowing us a clear month to tackle the arduous task of packing up and moving out of our work, home, etc. For Ali and Tim, her faithful and trustworthy fiancé, flying on Christmas Day to their dream honeymoon destination in the sunny south of Egypt meant they could take advantage of the low prices on offer and enjoy the convenience of airports and a plane not bogged down with congestion.

We had always hoped for a magical wedding day for our only daughter, but somehow the event managed to surpass even these high expectations. The festive red-and-white colour scheme suited the bride perfectly and brought a seasonal warmth and brightness to the beautifully decorated church and two reception venues.

The service itself was full of festive joy. As we sang our praises, we were accompanied by a set of the most accomplished and inspiring young musicians, with whom the bridal pair had played and sung many times previously. The result was the most moving and uplifting worship service I had attended in a good while. As we exited to Mariah Carey's 'All I Want for Christmas Is You', it was an excellent conclusion to the Yuletide jubilation.

Reception number one was a few paces across the church vestibule to the sumptuously decorated hall. Our church family had worked hard. On top of turning a typically plain church hall into a splendid venue, they had produced a wonderful buffet meal fit for a king. It was humbling at the same time as affirming of their sacrificial love. For reception number two the happy couple had elected the very same South Lawn Hotel where we had celebrated our own nuptials twenty-six years previously. Again the place was resplendent and the feast abundant.

Now, one of the engaging characteristics that runs in the Herman blood is the 'blondeness' that has spawned so many jokes. In fact, although physically a brunette, poor Ali has received a double dose of such genes, her mother (who is physically blonde) also being given to frequent 'blonde' moments. It was no surprise then that as we lined up for the official welcome, my sister, Nicky, was heard to comment to the newlyweds, 'It's been a long day for you; you should sleep well tonight!'

Later, as I proudly delivered my speech, extolling my daughter's many virtues and expressing my delight in receiving our wonderful new son-in-law, I complimented them both on their impeccable organisation of the accompanying festivities. 'It's the best wedding I've been to in twenty-six years!'

Sue, who'd been sitting at my side and drinking in every word, along with a modicum of bridal bubbly, was clearly taken aback by these words. 'What about ours?' she loudly exclaimed.

The assembled company exploded into laughter as she illustrated perfectly the play I had been making throughout the speech, that although Ali's hair was brown and was even her new surname, inside she was still as blonde as her charming mother.

The new year saw Jonna packing his bags for Bolivia in the company of his good friend Sam, with whom he had grown up. They were to spend time helping the missionary family sent out from our church and working with the many street children living in the highways and byways of the capital, La Paz. The next six months were complicated right from the kick-off. As he checked in at the airport, the counter staff queried his length of stay. The normal procedure would have been to take a bus trip over the border to renew his three-month visa halfway through. However, the person on duty was not having any of it, insisting that, in order to guarantee his timely exit from the country, Jonna should book an expensive air ticket instead!

Once he had arrived and was overcoming the attendant altitude sickness, the despair among the people he had gone to help was the next challenge to his determination to make a difference. 'It's like there's nobody there when you look into their eyes; they're all permanently high on glue', he told me over the phone soon after his arrival. Nonetheless, the children enjoyed Sam and Jonna's attention as they brought them a bit of cheer through various activities, including playing soccer and teaching them songs.

Events continued to conspire against Jonna's plans. Two weeks into his stay, he found himself confronted by a group of young men threatening to slit his throat and was forced to hand over his valuables. Then, two weeks later, he came down with typhus, which led to an uncomfortable stay in hospital and a debilitation that continued to dog him many months after his eventual return to England.

As well as embarking on married life, Ali was settling into her first year as a primary school teacher. To add to this challenging profession, she had plenty of difficult children to deal with, the school being located in one of the most deprived backwaters of Her Majesty's kingdom. In addition to that, the behaviour of her head and deputy was at times as childish and outrageous as any of their young charges. But Ali took it all in her stride and often had us in stitches with her Joyce Grenfell-like reports of awkward children and troublesome teachers.

CHAPTER 3

Driving Me Crazy

As I'VE ALREADY SAID, the early months at Betel were particularly taxing for Sue, who found herself completely at sea in our new environment. Living in someone else's home, adrift from family and friends, with no job, unfamiliar with the language, no confidence to drive on the wrong side of the road in a foreign country … it's a long list! Of course Mark and Julie did their best to make us comfortable. Our 'bed-sit' had everything we needed—it just wasn't ours; all our possessions were packed away into sixty-four boxes piled up in the 'chapel'. It didn't stop Sue mourning the loss of her own nest.

For the previous twenty-two years, we had lived in just one house; we'd renovated it and extended it to meet the needs of our growing family. Together we had put down our roots in a place where we were at ease, had all we needed to hand, and could find relaxation and rest. It hadn't been simply a matter of disposing of a prime piece of real estate but a proper bereavement as we left behind our family home, with every corner full of the memories of our freshly flown offspring. On top of that, we had not been the best at throwing things out, so it was all the more painful and horrible having to hurl one precious object after another into the bottom of a dirty old skip at the local rubbish tip.

As Jonna looked on, he summed up our sadness: 'Mum, Dad! You're throwing away my childhood!'

Then there were the memories of the times we had spent with the many dear friends who had sat snugly with us round the kitchen table, sipping coffee or enjoying the tasty results of Sue's legendary culinary skills in the form of a splendid dinner. On one occasion, we had just been across *La Manche*, the English Channel, taking advantage of the latest special offer from one of the local ferry companies to spend twenty-four hours in France catching up with *Les Copains*, our friends in Cherbourg, and filling the boot with delicious French fare.

As soon as we got home, we couldn't wait to celebrate and share these good things with some of our best friends back in *notre royaume*, our kingdom, as it were. These were pals who had accompanied us on previous trips, so we knew they would appreciate the sumptuous spread! Carefully we laid out the cheeses, including a ripe, soft, creamy Brie with a perfect mushroomy crust together with our favourite bargain red wine *Vieux Papes* with its rich, warm red palate, and the bread.

Surprisingly, it was the latter that attracted the most praise and appreciation from our guests. 'Nobody makes bread like the French do!' they chimed admiringly. The only problem was that real French bread is great on the day it's baked but invariably stale by the following morning, which meant that the acclaimed baguettes had in reality been freshly purchased just outside town, where Monsieur Tesco baked them on the premises! Of course, in our very English way, not wishing to shatter their illusion or cause any embarrassment, we heartily agreed!

As we tuned in to the Spanish radio during those early months, there were two songs that were played with great frequency and which became very meaningful to us: Bono's 'One' and a catchy Spanish-language hit called 'Nada Fue un Error', meaning 'It Was No Mistake'. The latter immediately became a firm favourite.

Sue identified closely with the emotional pain expressed in Bono's song. She still recalls the anguish vividly.

'The overriding feeling was the frustration; Bono's line about lepers in your head. Well, you remember, I screamed once. The frustration was awful, almost unbearable; it was agonising, because I was so powerless, and at times the feelings were frightening because they were so intense. And I was powerless and helpless in my own mind'.

She listed all the things that had been taken away from her. 'I am the sort of person who always likes to be in control, and all control had been taken from me. Yet at the same time, I knew we were in the right place, and it was trying to reconcile that with the awful feelings I had.

'Then on better days, when we heard 'Nada Fue un Error', I would feel more positive. I had very negative times and very positive times at the beginning. I very rarely had a normal, steady day until I had settled into a decent job, really. I guess I had some steady days, but not that many'.

We had now embarked on a new adventure and were sampling some of the rough side of life away from our homeland. We were on a steep learning curve! I was realising what I had recently learned from as study published in the Spanish press, that an important factor in a man's happiness is the happiness of his wife. The dream quality that had accompanied me so far was evaporating quickly. The rubber had hit the road and was causing a nasty burning smell.

Nevertheless, the excitement of following our calling kept us going, and while we looked forward to finding a new home of our own, we were enjoying getting to know our new friends Mark and Julie above all.

*　　*　　*　　*　　*

We were also discovering the diverse beauty of our new island home. It is quite possible to drive from one end to the other within an hour. Indeed, we have done it when visiting Phil, winding the last few kilometres up the steep mountainside to his highly distinguished, spacious residence just inside the sixty minute mark, to gain a bird's-eye view of the north coast. However, the smallest of diversions from the main arterial roads running north and south from Arrecife reveal the richness of the UNESCO Biosphere Reserve, which encapsulates all 326 square miles of the island and its attendant islets.

Starting on the south coast, Playa Blanca retains the charm of an attractive fishing village that has grown into a bustling resort. As the driver heads north, he is presented with a large variety of towns, villages, and monuments worth a stop. For example, the holiday town of Costa Teguise, lying just beyond Arrecife, is purpose-built, with its wide esplanade bordering the white sandy beaches, ideal for an evening *paseo*, or stroll. Although one is now just into the northern half of the isle, a decisive change in the character of the landscape occurs a little farther up the coast on leaving Arrieta, an unspoiled little fishing village with a rocky shoreline, reminiscent of the Greek islands.

This is the beginning of the *Malpaís*, or Badlands. As the name suggests, it is not fit for agricultural use. The large area of barren rocks is sprinkled with lichen in its subtle palette of pale blue-green colours. The few endemic plants to flourish rely cleverly on the lizards and birds one step up from them on the food chain to guarantee their survival.

The older towns, that is, the ones that are not purpose-built holiday resorts, have developed in typical Canarian style. They all appear to have started with the church and the town square and a few dwellings. As time has gone by, each 'pueblo' has been added to in random fashion, and it seems that once it became time to lay roads, it was a matter of tracing a track through the narrow gaps between the individual houses.

Arrecife is typical of this tendency. Hence, as I already mentioned, my first impression of the island's capital was of a confusing rabbit warren of streets.

The former capital, Teguise, lies a ten minute drive inland from its modern replacement, and is famous for its Sunday market. The extended display of stalls smothers the ancient town, filling the square in front of the church and radiating outwards through the surrounding streets, and the influx of tourists can only be described as massive. We normally manage to leave our home in Playa Blanca shortly after 9.30 to get to the shopping centre in Puerto del Carmen, where our church has its premises, in time to set up for our 11.00 a.m. meeting. We only have to leave a few minutes later, and the road becomes a long train of coaches heading north to the tourist Mecca, leaving us with no choice except to tag on the end and resign ourselves reluctantly to a late arrival.

I hate markets, but on April 1 a bit of folly seemed appropriate, and as a concession to Sue, I agreed to accompany her for a bit of 'retail therapy'. Thankfully we were constrained by the time of the church service to make a quick visit. Having arrived just as the market opened at 9.30, we were able to enjoy a quiet half hour browsing the displays in search of unusual birthday and Christmas presents. Every kind of souvenir was on offer alongside all sorts of crafts.

The huge central section of the market was devoted to all sorts of food at exorbitant prices. Whether you regard the extraordinary variety and cosmopolitan nature of these outlets as a redeeming feature or not could be a matter of debate. I had to admit it was quite a spectacle. I enjoyed the sight of so many different colours and textures and snapped up a few quick shots with my camera. What struck me most was the strange juxtaposition of the sublime tradition of the ancient craftsmanship and tacky 'sophistication' of the latest toys and trinkets.

One stand after another was offering the same repetitive range of items. Endless tables full of handbags, leather goods, fake Rolex watches, and interminable ranks of natural cotton clothing were punctuated by stalls selling plants and local produce. But our destination was a particular stall that had been recommended, where we were aiming to pick up some quality items of silver jewellery at very reasonable rates for family Christmas and birthday presents. Sue had even practised her Spanish phrases in order to give her newly acquired language skills an outing.

Having executed our purchases with pleasing precision and timeliness, we turned to leave. It was just approaching ten o'clock. As we headed back to the car, we glanced uphill toward the many temporary car parks set up in the fields around the town, to see a dark tide of people already swelling toward us. Soon it would engulf the whole metropolis.

'Phew! I'm glad we missed that', I commented.

We made our getaway feeling very satisfied—Sue with her purchases and successful use of the lingo, and me with the brevity of our stay. The only disadvantage of the early foray was that we were only able to hear the first few minutes of the band of Bolivian pan pipers, who completed the atmosphere as they filled the air with the soaring sounds of their mellow tunes.

'Thank you; I know how much you hate markets!' Sue said. 'I really appreciate your taking me; it means such a lot!'

Notwithstanding this positive experience, I still cannot help but marvel at the willingness of so many people to spend their Sunday morning in the last place that I would choose to go at any time of the week, let alone trade in the opportunity to receive a spiritual shot in the arm in one of our inspirational meetings. But then I'm thoroughly biased, of course!

*　　*　　*　　*　　*

At that time, a regular feature of our Sunday morning meetings was the presence of one or two homeless men, who would normally stagger in smelling of drink. They were of course given the same warm welcome as everyone else. Matthew was one of these. The quiet German had been appearing for a few weeks when Pastor Mark got a call from the hospital. They had found his number on Matthew's phone. It turned out that the unfortunate Matthew had been riding his bike when he lost control and took a tumble, ending up with a concussion and a nasty gash across his forehead.

Soon Mark and Julie had taken him in, giving him a home at Betel. Matthew declared his faith in Christ and that he would not touch a drop of liquor ever again. The long dusty road from Betel to the nearest civilisation, together with the absence of transport, would hopefully combine to encourage Matthew's adherence to his vow of abstinence.

A few weeks later it was time for our first visitor, Sue's mum. As we took the opportunity to escape from the bone-chilling Betel nights, we stayed in the same complex in Costa Teguise that we'd patronised the previous year. For one glorious week we lived like tourists, enjoying the warmth of the coastal resort. Along with the welcome warmth, we relished the space for ourselves and the chance to spend time with my sweet mother-in-law. We had already enjoyed the warm hospitality of a retired British couple, Ken and Jo, who lived close to where we were staying. They had even recommended the resort. Another top tip they had passed on was what turned out to be the best restaurant on the island—Las Maretas. Run by its unassuming and respectful proprietor, Domingo, this treasure is hidden away behind the main Las Cucharas beach in Costa Teguise.

Ken and Jo had highlighted the wonderful Baked Alaska. Our first visit saw us gladly complying with this recommendation, each managing to devour a delicious mountain of ice cream and sponge cake soaked in amaretto and covered in meringue. The only problem was my greed; the feeling that my stomach was about to explode into my chest coupled with a pervasive sense of nausea is something I will never forget! Future visits found us sharing one 'montaña blanca' between us. Domingo soon cottoned on to our nickname for the gigantic pudding, which we had renamed after a feature of the local landscape.

So when Sue's mum offered to pay for a meal out, there was no debate about the destination. The obliging Domingo was especially attentive and made sure our visitor's gastronomic experience was every bit as pleasant as we had led her to expect. As we came to order dessert, he posed the question that was to become habitual at that point in the proceedings: '¿Una montaña blanca y dos cucharas?' ('One montaña blanca and two spoons?') My lady companions both surprised me as they responded swiftly, Sue with a negative and her mum with an affirmative. My surprise turned to astonishment as my partner in pudding assassination devoured her half of the mountain at a breath-taking speed, thus demonstrating a mammoth appetite that her slender frame belied.

We returned to Betel refreshed and glad to find Matthew more happily settled and making good progress. He'd been attending meetings and lapping up the church's teaching. The greatest difficulty we had was getting him to simply talk. Without any drink inside him, he was so painfully shy and quiet. Given his progress, the events that unfolded came as a surprise and disappointment. One morning, when the rest of us were out, the desire for alcohol must have become too much. Having propelled him along the rocky path, down the main road, and into San Bartolomé, it led him to fill his skin with drink before he somehow found his way back home. When Mark and Julie returned, they found Matthew in a heap on the bathroom floor, having struck his head yet again. Clearly he needed a more secure environment in which to dry out and spiritually grow.

Thankfully the island was home to an excellent rehab centre called AUNAR. The home to a dozen recovering alcoholics and drug addicts lay a couple of miles north of Arrecife on the road to Tahiche. The obliging director, Carmelo, was ready with a friendly welcome for Matthew.

Finding AUNAR was relatively straightforward, compared to negotiating the confusing layout of streets in places like Arrecife and Teguise. Nonetheless, I was still struggling with the unfamiliar roads. As a Brit, I'm used to driving on the left. Therefore, the first thing I had to consider when attempting to navigate some of the most notoriously dangerous roads in the whole of Spain was keeping to the correct side of the carriageway. It could be partly my dyslexia coming into play here, because I was surprised that, after three months of setting off on the right-hand side of the road every day, it still felt completely unnatural.

In search of some reassurance, I confidently consulted my fellow dyslexic and good friend Mark, quite certain that he would have a similar story to tell. There would be the satisfying and reassuring conclusion that, despite the long period of adjustment, suddenly one day the proverbial penny had dropped. Nothing could have been further from the truth! My surprise deepened to alarm as I learned that he had taken to the 'wrong side' of the road like a duck to water!

On these occasions, I found one tip I'd been given invaluable. Whenever disorientation strikes, the simple solution is to check one's position vis-à-vis the centre of the road. If the driver should find themselves on the off side, their urgent priority is to veer swiftly 'onside' in order to avoid the feared collision with any oncoming traffic.

Most of the remaining challenges have to do with the rare creatures that inhabit these parts and can sometimes suddenly appear in the driver's field of view, causing anything from mild alarm to potentially fatal obstruction. In short, one needs to stay alert at all times. The first rare creature to be on the lookout for is the 'local loco'. They may be few and far between, but encountering such a beast is an experience not easily forgotten. Thankfully, I kept accident free in our first few months. It was a new friend, Alan, who had a disastrous encounter.

It was just before Easter that he was innocently making his way one morning around ten o'clock, up the hill from the small town of Guïme toward Montaña Blanca. Guïme, being well placed for the airport, a good number of British and Germans have purchased some magnificent villas there, perched on the hillside with panoramic views over the coast and airport a thousand feet below.

Without warning, a rogue vehicle loomed in Alan's path. The distinctive small green car had crossed the continuous white centre line to hurry past a little old truck and straight toward him. My friend had no choice but to steer off the road, his car bouncing over the rocky ground and somersaulting onto its roof. He miraculously climbed out of the upended piece of scrap into which his car had instantly been converted and walked away shaken but unscathed, apart from the odd bruise.

The reason that I can recount the incident in such vivid detail is that it fell to me to accompany the shattered Alan to the local police in order to interpret. This was in fact, the first time I had been called upon to translate. I was just extremely grateful that, as the Spanish say, 'No había que lamentar daños personales'—there were no personal damages to be lamented—my new friend hadn't been hurt physically. Nonetheless, he had now lost the sole means of getting himself and his tools to his building work, spread around the island.

The local police, otherwise known as the 'blue police', were unable to help, referring us instead to the Guardia Civil, a.k.a. the 'green police'. The colours are those that dominate their uniforms and vehicles, and the terms were coined by an engineering friend of ours. The green guys deal with the roads outside town. Accordingly, an hour or so from the start of our quest for justice, we walked apprehensively into the cuartel of the still militarised, gun-toting, and rather formidable Guardia. If I hadn't been my friend's only option, I may well not have had the courage to cross the threshold.

In the end, my anxiety was unfounded. The two gentlemen who

attended us were the embodiment of charm, sympathy, and helpfulness. As Alan told the sorry story once more, they listened intently and clarified every detail, including the way his truck had flipped 'head over heels', translating to *vuelco de campana*, literally 'overturning bell'. In the meantime, they were keen to compare notes about England. They talked about the places they had visited and asked where we had lived. The New Forest fascinated and astounded them. They simply could not comprehend how semi-wild ponies could be allowed to roam the roads freely. Weren't there a lot of accidents? I told them we Brits drive more slowly, so it wasn't really a problem!

Having made a detailed report, to my surprise, they jumped into their 4x4 and instructed me to lead them to Alan's house. What nerves I had, driving with the police tailing me all the way from Arrecife to Tías, one of the longest fifteen-minute periods of my life so far! The most tense moment was as we turned into Alan's street. Officially it was a 'no left turn', but here things like that are regularly ignored. What should I do? Thankfully, Alan had the presence of mind to make a simple gesture to the gentlemen behind us that established within milliseconds that we had their permission to make the thoroughly normal, though illegal, manoeuvre!

The state of Alan's vehicle was impressive. I was marvelling at how he had survived, and so were the Guardia. Out came the digital camera to collect photographic evidence. Having established Alan's erstwhile mode of transport as a write-off, we then drove another nerve-wracking ten minutes to the scene of the crime. Now the photos were being taken of the tell-tale tracks that started as clear skid marks on the tarmac and disappeared quickly into the robust rocky landscape. The tumbling metal missile had hardly disturbed the far tougher terrain. The former had definitely come off worse!

I think that was probably the final straw for Alan and his wife, Margaret; it was soon after that they returned to live in England. For me it was a valuable experience that gave me confidence that I could approach the police on behalf of my needy compatriots, communicate successfully, and find real interest and support, even if, as in this case, the culprit was never found. The most important lesson of all was to keep one's wits about one at all times. 'Local locos' can appear at any moment, especially when they're least expected.

CHAPTER 4

An Englishman's Home Is His Castle

As SOON AS OUR bags were unpacked, we set about finding work. Before that we needed to acquire the infamous NIF. The *numero de identificación fiscal* is more or less the equivalent of the national insurance number in the United Kingdom or social security number in the United States. Having freshly arrived, and knowing nothing, we engaged the services of a local paperwork buster to get our NIFs for us. As he took our money and gave us some free tips about life in Lanzarote, he finished off with a striking caveat: 'But don't believe me. In fact, don't believe anything anybody ever tells you here!'

I confess I found this statement completely baffling. Why would anybody offer sincere advice and then round it off with what appeared to amount to a wholesale retraction? And why shouldn't we believe him anyway? Everyone else seemed to implicitly trust his advice! I continued to puzzle over the issue during the following months.

The next thing was the language, which Sue had been learning in England, albeit at a rather basic level. She decided to investigate the possibility of an intensive course at a local language school. As she phoned the Merlin school in Playa Honda, a ten-minute drive down the hill, she discovered that they taught English and consequently found a few hours' work there. Her first students were two young Spanish mothers learning the basics.

With the financial support we were getting from our friends and family in England, and the euro being a lot cheaper than it is now, I was able to dedicate half my working day to the church. I continued to shadow Mark, learning how to prepare sermons and accompanying him on pastoral visits. The biggest concern was Paula, since the return of her cancer had been confirmed. She would now be treated with her own stem cells. Thankfully the treatment was successful and the disease retreated once more.

I needed to find some paid work to fill the other half of my working day. The obvious skill to exploit was my ability with the Spanish language, translating and interpreting. At the same time, we were looking at houses in Playa Blanca. The agent showing us around turned out to be the most honest and genuinely pleasant person—totally the opposite of what we expected from a man in his line of business! As he drove us around, we got to chatting about life on the island and work in particular.

'My wife runs a wedding planning business. I'll ask if she needs any help translating', he volunteered.

In my anxiety to get going, I kept taking out my cell phone and examining it to make sure I hadn't missed a vital call. At the same time I was counselling myself not to be so impatient and unrealistic. When the phone rang the very next morning, I wondered who it could be.

'Hi, is that Chris? It's Sally, Richard's wife. You remember yesterday he was showing you some properties in Playa Blanca?'

It struck me as a funny question in the light of the fact that I had hardly been able to think about anything else since then! Sally and her business partner, Dawn, were organising a wedding to take place in Teguise in two weeks' time. They needed the service translated from the Spanish, and the priest needed an interpreter by his side for the big day. Naturally lacking in confidence and still a bit nervous about the whole business, I was nevertheless very excited.

The context was a church in Teguise, the favourite spot for betrothed couples to tie the knot in Lanzarote. La Villa de Teguise, to give the town its full name, provides a beautiful stage for these ceremonies. Archaeologists believe the first settlement in the whole of the Canaries was established here, with recent evidence pointing to its having been inhabited as early as 1,000 BC.

As I approached from the south and the road led me through a wide plane, I couldn't help but be impacted again with the grandiose beauty of the island. Glancing to my left I glimpsed the coast and a view of the spectacular cliffs of Famara in the distance. The upward slope toward the town became ever steeper in its final kilometre before entering the ancient fortress capital with its commanding views over the entire island.

It was quite a different experience from the one I'd had a few weeks previously when my focus was on raiding the gigantic weekly Sunday market before the invasion of masses of tourists. This time I was able to appreciate some of the finest buildings and the most impressive traditional colonial architecture on the island. I found the Church of Nuestra Señora de Guadalupe standing proudly in the middle, adorning the picturesque Teguise Square. As I stepped through the door framed by red quarry stone, I discovered a wonderful blend of mediaeval artwork and Canarian design. The three neo-Gothic-style naves and impressive proportions gave it the feel of a proper cathedral.

Ten minutes before the celebration was due to start, I took my place next to the priest at the front of the magnificent sanctuary, facing the assembled wedding party. As the service started, the beautiful bride took her place beside us, trembling almost imperceptibly with nerves, with the proud groom next to her.

Everything started smoothly. The readings were read, the hymns were sung, and a cousin of the bride rendered a spine-tingling performance of the Lord's Prayer sung in Gaelic to a melody that resonated around the old auditorium as if it had been made for it. Then it came for the critical moment when the rings were to be exchanged.

First the groom was to place the symbolic circle of gold on his bride's finger. Now, bear in mind that all this takes place, not as in the weddings I've been to in England, with their backs to the onlookers, but high up and facing the dearly beloved gathered to witness. In full view of the whole assembly, the groom hesitated and whispered to me in a panic, 'Which finger?'

In the heat of the moment, and feeling an awesome sense of responsibility, all sorts of thoughts went through my mind. *Well, I wear mine on my left hand. But they are Irish, so it could be the other way round. And they're Catholic, so that may be different again.* Looking back on the confusion of the moment, I'm sure the hesitation wasn't nearly as long as it seemed. As a ripple of subdued laughter ran through the assembled company, he quickly chose the correct finger and regained his composure. Nonetheless, the funniest part was still to come. As the blushing bride's turn came to repeat the identical vows and movements, she hesitated at exactly the same point!

As I repeated my translation of the priest's words into English, it felt for all the world as if I was the one doing the marrying, especially when it came to the part where the clergyman turned to me discreetly and whispered, 'If you like, you can tell them that at this point they are free to embrace one another'. The newlyweds looked at me with nervous expectancy, wondering what might have gone wrong. So it was a delightful duty to pronounce those climactic words, 'You may now kiss the bride!'

If variety is the spice of life, then my working life in Lanzarote was promising to be a very interesting mixture of exotic spices, some more pleasant than others. Overall though, I was enjoying working with people, as opposed to sitting behind a desk and staring at a computer screen all day. It was hard to believe I had put up with that for twenty-three years!

* * * * *

Exactly two days after our arrival, we had been delighted to find the perfect vehicle for our use—a second-hand Peugeot Diesel 106, a real rarity, especially here where the supply of used cars is so restricted due to the diminutive size of the island. We had immediately set about searching for a house of our own. Our first thought had been Tías, the medium-sized town that sits a short drive up the hill from Puerto del Carmen and the church where I was working. Sue had always wanted to live in a house with a view, and Tías is full of them, so it seemed to us just the right place. The only trouble was there was just nothing available that suited us at the right price.

As we spread the net wider, none of the houses we were shown really appealed. Finally, just two weeks after we set foot on 'the rock' we attended our first meeting for the pastors and wives from our group of churches. There were six couples around the table and the whole thing was conducted in Spanish. The other people there were all very welcoming and keen to help us settle in, and in particular Carlos and Tina, who worked as estate agents. In the days that followed they showed us a number of different properties; but they turned out to be less to our taste than ever. In the end, they persuaded us to accompany them to the very bottom of the island, a half-hour drive from where we had started to look, to the up-and-coming coastal resort of Playa Blanca, which has since become the most popular on Lanzarote.

Our very first visit to Playa Blanca had been when our friends Guy and Hazel were taking their customary two-week spring break in a timeshare villa on a beautiful complex called Las Brisas, located just across the road from the pedestrian shopping precinct that backs onto the long promenade. At the eastern end of the precinct stands 'the anchor' roundabout, acting as a handy reference point with its large and prominent artefact sitting proudly in the middle. It also serves as a convenient drop-off point for punters like ourselves going for an evening *paseo* along the promenade and a bite to eat. As we crossed a little plaza from there to the seafront, I immediately succumbed to the hypnotic tranquillity. A profoundly relaxing atmosphere was being generated, with the hubbub of holidaymakers enjoying their meals in a long string of restaurants spilling out onto one side of the paved walkway, and the sea lapping lazily against the rocks on the other. The lights of the adjacent harbour completed the serenity of the scene, casting their warm glow across the darkened waters of the bay.

Our next visit was in the cheerful company of Carlos and Tina. As we toured the town looking at different properties, we were joined by Hugo, the Colombian pastor from Playa Blanca, whom I had got to know during my first visit to the island. His wife, Amanda, was with him. They were very happy because they were soon to move in to a brand-new house, and become homeowners for the first time since emigrating from Colombia five years previously.

Hugo reminded me of the Mario cartoon character: short and slightly tubby with a black moustache riding on his habitual smile. This jolly character always greeted me with the affection of a long-lost brother coupled with great respect: '¡Hola, Chris!, ¿Cómo estás? ¡Qué alegría de verte!' ('Hi, Chris, how are you? Great to see you!') One time he made me forget where I was, so effusive was his welcome, that I went to kiss him as if we were in France. He happily returned the embrace without the least bit of embarrassment. *Oh well,* I thought, *the Bible does tell us to greet one another with a holy kiss!* It was hard to believe he had been a violent drug dealer before his conversion to Christianity.

Having been shown a rather small villa located on a holiday complex, we crossed the road to the smart, newly built estate where Hugo and Amanda's new home was situated. The semi-detached building, comprising a small kitchen, lounge, two bedrooms, and two bathrooms covered an area of fifty square metres, a mere tenth of the large plot, and came with its own swimming pool. The accommodation surrounded two sides of a huge courtyard, while a gigantic carport made a third side. It was very much a modern variety of the traditional Spanish home in the sun, a beautiful example of what the Spanish would call *una casa muy blanca,* literally *a very white house,* standing squarely and pristinely with its flat roof and whitewashed walls reflecting the sunshine with blinding brightness. In this case, the effect was cleverly enhanced by large areas of smoke-coloured tinted glass, framed in glossy marine-blue aluminium, thus maintaining the traditional values of the typical Spanish home while updating them with an ultramodern finish.

Hugo showed me round, enthusing excitedly about all his plans for extending and altering the house. The house in Hugo's imagination was twice as big as the one in front of us. By covering over the courtyard, he was going to create an enormous living room, while the carport would be converted into a massive master bedroom fit for a king and his queen.

I must just explain at this point that the way houses are built here is that they are half-built. The builder leaves the new owner with numerous opportunities to do what they call *cerrar,* which means to close, or *tapar,* to put a lid on, thereby increasing the size of the living area. They leave spaces such as an expansive courtyard, or a huge car port, ready prepared with power points and even lighting cables hanging out of the wall. One only has to *cerrar* or *tapar* and *¡ya está!,* there you have it!

I couldn't believe Hugo wanted to cover the whole of his courtyard. The beauty of the time honoured central patio is that it allows the entry of pleasant breezes during the hotter months, stopping the home becoming an oven. In the winter, the sun shining through the large patio doors provides welcome warmth and combines with the ventilation to prevent dampness. Nevertheless, I could appreciate the attraction of the home with all its space and potential, so that when it transpired that there was one house left for sale just a couple of doors down from our friends, my imagination was already fired up.

Like Hugo, I could see the house as it would be after we'd closed in and roofed over the appropriate areas. To me, the immaculate, high-spec home, nestling into the red mountainside on the smart estate of sixty-four similarly equipped dwellings, was a real find. I could clearly see how well the house would meet our needs with half the courtyard taken to complete a beautiful lounge diner, and the car port transformed into a large square double bedroom for ourselves. The picture was finished by a modest extension of the kitchen. The potential outside matched that of the interior living space, the extraordinary climate lending itself to the creation of a delightful garden full of all kinds of lush tropical plants and brightly coloured flowers. The trouble was that, although *I* could envisage all these exciting facilities, Sue simply saw a rabbit hutch surrounded by lots of grey volcanic grit. She was completely despondent.

A few days after our first visit, our good friends Guy and Hazel arrived for a holiday. Naturally, the first thing on our agenda was to show them the contentious candidate for our new home. As they toured the site and examined it carefully, Guy expressed complete solidarity with my view, while Hazel took Sue's side. As we looked on, a startling argument ensued. It started shortly after we arrived for the inspection, grew in intensity as we showed them around, and was still going full pelt as we left them at their villa an hour later. This extraordinary intervention was surprisingly helpful. We didn't need to argue ourselves; our friends were doing it in our place! The funniest thing was that, at the end of it all, Hazel texted all our mutual friends in England with an emotional report that created such a stir that some of them even started to worry that we might be about to break up over the issue! Eventually, after several attempts at transferring my mental plans to paper and hours of discussion, I managed to communicate my vision, and Sue came round to my way of thinking. That was a month to the day after our arrival.

The next step was to get the necessary finance together. Carlos and Tina, enthusiastically supported by Hugo and Amanda, presented us with great anticipation to the manager of the local bank. A 'very nice man' and personal friend of Amanda's, Ramón represented a one-stop solution to our housing provision. He was both selling the house and offering a small mortgage to enable us to extend it immediately in any way we wished, free of planning permission, as long as we stayed within the original 'footprint'.

The only thing lacking was the paperwork, which would all be complete within the month. This was music to our ears; we'd be safely installed by the middle of the merry month of May. Having been in a state of upheaval and without a place to call our home for just over two months, we were most definitely ready to relocate to a new place we could call our own, above all after the inconveniences of life at Betel. Things were going well!

One of the many differences in the whole process of house buying here is the role of the legal beagles. Being used to, and feeling therefore more secure with, 'the British way' of employing a solicitor for such an important transaction, we followed Ramón's recommendation and engaged the services of the distinguished Jorge, a man who was very clear in his communication and reassuring in his explanation of the paperwork that needed attention. Our warm feeling was further increased by his glowing affirmation of the architect and builder as an 'efficient' man.

The following weeks and months seemed to go on forever. Up and down, round and round, we alternated visits to Ramón at the bank with phone calls to Jorge. Ramón was a very nice man indeed, always leaving us heartily encouraged that 'in a couple of weeks' the house would be ours. These visits would be followed ten days or so later by a call to our solicitor friend, who was turning out to be a man with an appropriate, if rather depressing sense of irony, as he dryly and crisply redefined Ramón's reassuring words. 'The house will be yours in a couple of weeks just means that it is not yet yours and that it will continue to not be yours for an undefined period of time'.

In summary, this was a testing time for our belief that our property purchase was in line with our vocation. The problem was that the tide of time was going out and we were having visions of being stranded at Betel and unable to look after our basic needs for water and electricity. Mark and Julie were also buying a home and soon had a completion date. Once they were gone, we would be unable to manage the cranky old generator that was an indispensable source of power for pumping the water and lighting the dark old building.

At this point of near exasperation with life in the slow and bumpy lane at Betel, and weary of waiting, we were wonderfully relieved to receive our first visit from my mum and her partner, Christopher. For two balmy weeks we tried to relax and become tourists. During that fortnight of escape we occupied two well-appointed holiday apartments, situated in a quiet corner of a beautifully kept complex in Playa Blanca. It was a quick hop over a low volcanic stone wall and scramble down a short bank onto a tranquil stretch of the ten mile promenade that snakes its way along the sea front, starting from Papagayo in the east to the Faro lighthouse in the west, perched watchfully on the tip of its own promontory.

*   *   *   *   *

At the start of July 2006, as we returned to Betel, Mark and Julie took the opportunity to escape for a long-overdue holiday, leaving us in charge of both the finca and the church. Four days after their departure, we were enjoying a barbecue with friends in their house in San Bartolomé, the next town up from Güime, with its extensive view over the southeast coast, including the busy airport.

The festivities were just reaching their peak when my phone rang. On the other end was a man named Paul. In his late thirties, he had recently been attending church meetings, brought by his friend Terry. They were both of no fixed abode, spending their days foraging around the seafront for the odd beer or bag of chips. They spent their nights trying to get some sleep on the cold, damp sandy beach whilst endeavouring to hang on to the few possessions they carried with them, and which would otherwise have fallen prey to the prowling illegal immigrants from the nearby African continent.

Paul was in a panic. 'I think I'm having a heart attack!'

I quickly jumped in the car and hurried down to the coast where he was waiting. Previous experience of another emergency situation with a family member on holiday had taught me a valuable lesson: call for an ambulance! This way, the patient gets immediate attention, perceived as a stretcher case to be taken care of without delay. Anyone who arrives in the car is merely counted among the walking wounded.

Accordingly I dialled 112 and was relieved to see the Red Cross vehicle appear within a few minutes. They zoomed past us and came to a halt two hundred yards farther along the strip. I then had great difficulty in getting them to come back to us, which almost caused *me* a cardiac arrest. Finally the crew took charge of the frightened Paul. After some initial tests on the spot, they carried him off to the local clinic, with me driving behind, desperate not to lose contact. The next hour was one of the most alarming and bizarre I've had to live through in all my time here.

Paul was presented post-haste to the very strange-looking 'doctor', who looked for all the world as if he'd just been washed up on the beach himself. His very dark skin, bony face, and exaggerated jaw reminded me of textbook pictures of the first hominid to emerge from Africa eighty thousand years ago. As we sat across the desk from him, I couldn't help wondering if he'd stolen the white coat from a real doctor on the beach. Perhaps the coat's owner had been for a swim during his coffee break and returned to shore to find the garment gone. Meanwhile, the man was barking an interrogation at the unwitting patient while noisily chewing on some sort of nut.

The plot thickened as we moved to the examination room. We were ushered in by a very pleasant and professional-looking nurse, who turned out to be from Pamplona.

'It was the first bull run today, wasn't it?' I ventured, latching quickly on to the opportunity for some light conversation.

'That's right! It's so barbaric. I'm very glad to be here instead', she replied.

I couldn't help thinking that I would much prefer to be in Pamplona myself! The individual in the white coat was now fumbling with the wires and electrodes obviously designed to facilitate an ECG. He plainly hadn't a clue! Thankfully, Paul was on his back, and oblivious to both the spoken and body language taking place between the nurse on the one hand, and her highly contrasting colleague on the other. With my charge's interests at heart, the best thing I could think to do was to speak to him in reassuring tones so he could at least keep calm and, if the worst came to the worst, die peacefully!

Finally, the doctor's lack of patience turned in his subject's favour. He brusquely declared the equipment to be faulty and had Paul dispatched forthwith to the main José Molina Orosa Hospital in Arrecife.

Soon he was receiving the more competent care of a completely genuine-looking Spanish lady doctor. She speedily produced a set of leads identical to the ones recently announced as useless, and had them in place and functioning correctly in no time. *So that's how the other doctor should have attached them,* I thought.

Things were looking up. As the doctor asked what sort of pain Paul had been experiencing, I was even able to employ an expression I had just learned in my weekly conversation exchanges with a Spanish nurse. A sharp pain is described in Spanish as a *dolor de garra*—a clawing pain, with the accompanying gesture of the hand closing menacingly like the paw of a lion seizing its prey.

However pleased I was that finally Paul was having some serious attention, the doctor remained singularly unimpressed, particularly as she probed him about his alcohol intake. Soon we were dismissed with a couple of paracetamol for the pain. Although Paul was probably relieved, he also seemed understandably disappointed that they hadn't at least given him a bed for the night and kept him under observation.

Despite the recent setback with Matthew, I had no qualms about offering Paul a bed at Betel. I knew that Mark and Julie would have done the same. Over the next few days, Paul made himself at home with us, picking up a few more belongings from a mate's house in Tías, where he had previously taken shelter.

As Paul dried out, he told us how he had come to be living in such desperate circumstances. It all started when his business had gone belly up a year or so earlier. He had been a top chef, running a top-flight restaurant, frequented by the rich and famous, and situated in its own grounds on the outskirts of the village of Conil. 'Posh nosh in a restored finca', one diner had commented on the Internet. Unfortunately, with the stress of it all, he had been looking for solace in the twin addictions of gambling and alcohol. To cut a long story short, his wife finally kicked him out, and he ended up living rough on the beach.

The highlight of Paul's stay with us came one evening. As we chatted around the kitchen table, another piece of the crumbling ceiling hitting the table top somehow sparked the idea of setting Paul a *Ready Steady Cook*–style challenge. Our frugal means meant that rations were running low. As our guest ferreted around among the remaining food in the old gas fridge and searched the shelves and cupboard for herbs and spices, he found an interesting assortment of ingredients, from which he then proceeded to concoct the most amazing meal.

Following a carefully prepared starter of chicken mousse, Paul presented us with chicken breasts wrapped in Serrano ham, sitting proudly on a nest of finely sliced potatoes and complemented with exquisitely sculpted courgettes and carrots. This *plat de resistance* was finished off with a wonderfully tasty sauce, skilfully brewed up from an onion, some stock, and the remainder of an old carton of cream our chef had found hiding in the back of the fridge.

Okay, so the setting was not the most salubrious; but the ratio of quality to price was off the scale! Above all, it was a wonderful pleasure and surprise to see someone who had been in such a state a few days earlier, already recovering to the point where he was able to produce such a magical meal, in a similar fashion to the conjurer pulling the proverbial rabbit from the hat.

*   *   *   *   *

Ramón's final announcement of completion of our house purchase 'in a couple of weeks' was accompanied by more definite vocabulary such as *seguro* (sure) and *cierto* (certain). But sure and certain were two things that we seemed to have lost the capability of being, so much so that it came as quite a surprise when we got the phone call summoning us to attend the notary's office the next day. The whole thing seemed rather unreal as we drove to Arrecife and found our way to the office, where a whole crowd of people were attempting the same as we were—the exchange of contracts and completion of the purchase of a piece of property. It was all crammed into that one visit, everything the solicitors would do in a month or more in England.

The upside was that, as we sat and waited our turn, we met four lots of new neighbours, including those about to move in on either side of us. On one side at number fifty was to be Celina, a friendly Canarian lady of a similar age to ourselves. On the other side would be the soft-spoken Cristóbal, an equally friendly local taxi driver in his thirties with a big smile. Jimmy, an Englishman who had been living here for twenty-five years, was purchasing a home to share with his Spanish wife and two little boys. It was fun all being together and finding out what personable folks we were soon to share our street with. It reminded me of twenty-five years previously, when we bought our first house in England on a development built specifically for young first-time buyers.

They were exciting times as we transferred the money from the sale of our home ten thousand pounds at a time. Using a company that specialises in foreign-exchange transfers, we saved a little on the exchange rate and were served by our own personal dealer, making us feel very important. Every euro we made over our target of seventy pence each, we put aside to fund weekly escapes from Betel.

One of the costs at the notary was the virtually obligatory employment of a legal translator to the tune of one hundred euros. Our solicitor warned us sternly that our Spanish would have to be excellent to get away without one. *But you have explained the contract to us thoroughly; I can't see what the fuss is about,* I thought. *And the hundred euros is a lot of money.* I elected riskily to turn down the services of the Spanish expert, go it alone, and add one hundred euros to my special fund. The tension mounted as our turn came to enter the hallowed quarters of the notary himself, and the solicitor hissed his repeated warning through clenched teeth.

The notary, an exceedingly well-heeled young man, turned to us and uttered some introductory remarks. I froze with terror. His utterance was so fast that I found it completely incomprehensible! Struggling to overcome my paralysis, I muttered something vague in an attempt to cover up my ignorance. His retort was as short as it was unmistakable, '*¿Más o menos?*' ('More or less?') Then it dawned on me: he had simply asked us whether we could understand some simple Spanish. I responded immediately, '*Oh, sí sí sí*', nearly falling off my chair under the heady influence of a strange mixture of relief and embarrassment. My bet had paid off.

In the meantime, Matthew was making good progress at AUNAR. Every Wednesday morning I would pop in to spend half an hour catching up with him. It was really rewarding to see him recovering, and knowing that he was in a much safer environment than he had been at Betel. In addition, I loved the opportunity to employ my Spanish and German language skills to good effect. The former enabled me to communicate with the lively Carmelo, while the latter proved invaluable when Matthew reverted to his mother tongue, something he was apt to do from time to time for no particular reason that I could fathom. Unfortunately for Matthew, his Spanish language was virtually non-existent, which resulted in him feeling rather out of things.

Matthew was soon allowed to accompany us to Sunday meetings. Picking him up made for a bit of a detour; but we enjoyed those journeys, particularly because they proved a great way of helping Matthew to open up. I think he was more comfortable sitting beside me and not needing to give eye contact, and really appreciated the opportunity to converse in a language that he knew well, having been unable to communicate properly with another human being all week.

'There are some interesting characters living at AUNAR!' he exclaimed one morning as we drove along the open bypass that was taking us around the coastal sprawl of Puerto del Carmen before we would dip down into the old town where the church was located.

'There's one guy who's been there ten years. He is the comic of place. I can't understand a word he says; but he's still so funny! I can't imagine he'll ever leave'.

'*Max und Moritz dachten nun, was ist hier jetzt wohl zu tun?*' ('Max and Moritz thought, now what can we do here then?') I quoted a piece of my favourite German poetry.

'I think I'll be ready to leave soon. I want to go back to Munich, pick up my stuff, and bring it back here and do some work', was Matthew's response.

While I was glad Matthew was feeling so much better and was planning for a healthy future, it did strike me as a bit early for him to be leaving AUNAR. I'd been told that he should be thinking of a stay of a year or two. Matthew had been there just three months.

The very next Wednesday I was astonished as Matthew walked into our noon prayer meeting. Mark immediately took him by the shoulder and led him outside.

'What do you think you're doing? Are you crazy?'

'I'm fine', Matthew retorted. 'If I stay in that place any longer, I'll go crazy'.

Mark raised an imaginary bottle to his lips and acted out glugging it back. 'If you don't get back there at once, I guarantee that in six weeks you'll be back on the bottle!'

As for me, I was still hoping Mark would be proven wrong. It seemed to be a bit of a harsh prognostication. Matthew's reaction was to go into a sulk and run to Jane, one of the older ladies in the church who had adopted a motherly stance toward him. Sadly for us, she took offence when she heard how Mark had spoken to him and promptly left the church.

'That's one of the effects of having alcoholics among us. You've got to keep your eye out. Manipulation—they're masters of the art!'

Sure enough, and despite all our efforts to support him, Matthew sadly fell off the wagon a few weeks later.

*　　*　　*　　*　　*

Having our own home was a wonderful respite after the inconveniences of life at Betel and the long uncertain wait. One clear benefit would be the ability to communicate easily with our family at long last. Before we set sail on our journey here, we had comforted ourselves with the cheering notion that, as soon as we were into our own house, we would get on to Skype. With the aid of a webcam, we'd soon be enjoying frequent face-to-face chats with our nearest and dearest. It would be just as if they were in the next room rather than two thousand miles away. However, our new abode had no phone, and, as the initial waiting list of one month turned into two months, then six, any such expectations receded rapidly into oblivion.

The trouble was that, as is normal in this part of the world, we bought a newly built house. It is so normal that older houses are described as *segunda mano* (second hand). We were completely oblivious to the fact that the telephone cabling had not yet been laid and the normal delay before getting a phone was two long years. Not that they tell the householder that when they apply for it. Two weeks to a month is the standard promise. Repeated inquiries with the monopoly landline provider Telefonica via *mil cuatro* (1004) eventually end in the sudden disappearance of any record of the original application, and the bewildered potential customer is left to start again from scratch.

The lack of communication only served to underscore the separation from our family and friends back in England. It also became clear very quickly that the most distressing separation is that between a loving mother and her cherished children. The little communication we were able to have during this period was extremely expensive. As one friend commented to us sympathetically, the newly installed resident haemorrhages money for the first year or two of his or her life here. Added to that, our son was only reachable on his cell phone. The abysmally poor quality of the sound translated into great difficulty in understanding just about anything he said. It really was the pits. The only way we could console ourselves was to be thankful that at least we didn't have to rely on the post, another non-existent 'luxury' that we had taken so much for granted back in England.

Thus we struggled to keep up to date with Ali and Jonna, as their young adult lives matured quickly through all their new experiences. While we were opening a new chapter in our own lives, Ali had now been married for a little more than six months, and Jonna was learning first-hand how tough life can be in Bolivia.

For me as a father, although I was missing my children dearly, at the same time it was a delight to watch them growing in confidence and reaching the potential I had seen in them and helped to bring to fulfilment over the span of their young lives. Knowing they were out in the world, making their own unique and special contribution, gave me a particular sense of satisfaction. I always loved hearing their news and was glad of every opportunity to talk to them on the phone, even though sometimes it was frustratingly brief.

For their mother, however, things were more complicated. Telephonic communication being incomplete at the best of times, she would often feel profoundly dissatisfied at the end of a call, and the depression that descended upon her as a result would stay with her for days. My reaction was, and still is, rather different. I can often feel the sadness welling up to tears as the time to say good-bye approaches once again. Thankfully, my self-control was powerful enough to prevent me from melting into a weeping wreck while we were still talking. Once the phone went down, I would let the tears flow, and although it was uncomfortable for a few minutes, I found the consequent sense of release a real benefit.

Meanwhile, Sue's instinct to draw her offspring under her wings and give them protection and security was leading to a haunting anxiety coupled with a grinding guilt, a poisonous cocktail of emotion that wouldn't allow her to enter into the enjoyment of the positive points of our new life. The great majority of the other mums we knew here were also separated from their children, and suffering in the same way.

Typical of this was Margaret, married to Alan, who'd suffered the disastrous encounter with the local loco. They were a delight to have in our church, their attractively lilting Geordie accents complementing their lovely characters. Alan was an accomplished actor and wonderful comedian, who had appeared most famously in the successful TV series *Auf Wiedersehen Pet*. Sweet little Margaret stood out with her pretty blonde looks. I sat astonished as they told me stories of how they had remodelled their different homes, scarcely being able to believe that the petite Margaret had laboured for her husband as he capably took charge of the work. Sadly for us, the pull of family ties combined with Alan's car accident proved too much, and all too soon we were missing them both.

Along with the kids, Sue's thoughts frequently turned wistfully to all her other family and friends she had left behind, whose absence she felt acutely from her daily life—friends at church, childhood friends she'd known for thirty years and more, friends from work. Basically, she was keenly experiencing the downside of her sociable and caring nature. With texting being the only sensible means of keeping in touch, one evidence of this was the astronomical monthly cell phone bills! She had given up so much to support me in my vocation that I felt really mean even thinking of asking her to cut down. In the end, we just consigned it to the lengthening list of emotional and financial cost.

*   *   *   *   *

As soon as we were in, it was time to start the alterations to our new home. The first task was to create a sixteen square-foot bedroom out of the carport. We employed Mark's son, Ben, for the purpose. He immediately put his team to work, with scarcely four weeks until the room was needed to accommodate our first pair of eagerly awaited visitors, Tim and Ali. We had great fun as the men took up their tools. Dick, a jolly cockney bricklayer, and Alan, who had worked in construction as well as in show business. While Alan spent a whole day heroically felting the roof in the burning summer sun, Dick, having blocked up the walls, set about tiling the large expanse of floor area to perfection.

As the work progressed, we needed the kitchen patio door to be relocated into the new bedroom wall, thus allowing a view of and access to the internal garden this would become. On the outside wall we envisaged a large window looking out toward the Ajache mountains that divide the southern tail of the island from the central mass beyond. The kitchen was then to be extended a few feet beyond where the patio doors now stood, which involved a new window to sit above the new length of worktop.

These modifications required the services of the sort of carpenter who specialised in metalwork to match the original blue aluminium frames of the windows and patio doors. Since we were among the first few owners to take up residence, there weren't many neighbours to ask for a recommendation. But Ben had got the bit between his teeth! One sunny morning he ventured out into the neighbourhood and found, a few doors up from us, the first neighbour to have moved in and started work on completing his new home to his particular requirements. His name was Pedro and he happened to be in that morning because his work was at night in a local disco. 'Come and see what he's done!' Ben urged.

Pedro's alterations had involved a feature of the traditional Lanzarote home called the *solana*, a utility room without a roof. A drain in the centre of the terracotta tiled floor allows the dispersal of the infrequent precipitation of water from the normally blue skies. However sparse the fall of rain may be, though, one still feels instinctively that the resulting mixture of water and electricity could represent a potentially fatal hazard. Roofing over it would also allow the reliably dry storage of all sorts of useful kitchen and garden materials and implements. On inspection, we found our new friend had *tapado* (covered over) his solanas with a smart arrangement of white UPVC roof over long, narrow windows for ventilation.

The work had been carried out efficiently by an Argentinian for a good price. We immediately called the man for a quote, and he was soon installing all the necessary roofing and windows. We were really pleased to have found a good tradesman so quickly, and even happier when we realised that we had something special in common; we were both pastors of churches. Virgilio was a tall and burly, blustering man in his late forties with a thick moustache and an even thicker accent. It was really hard for me to understand, even with a good knowledge of Spanish. Fortunately we also shared a well-developed sense of humour and found much to laugh at in our clumsy communication. Thus we made new friends, and under Ben's careful supervision, the first phase was completed just in time.

A further attraction of the house was its proximity to a new all singing all dancing commercial centre. A few yards down the road and around the corner, was the site of the 'soon to be built' shopping and entertainment complex that was going to offer the best in retail and leisure experiences. It would enhance the living experience as well as the value of property—once it was completed, that is!

At the time of purchasing the house, the place was more like a bomb site. About 150 yards square, the first side we passed on our way home from the coast, was protected by a long stretch of corrugated iron fencing. As we turned left, uphill and past the second side of the site, the border appeared to be mainly a long white wall punctuated by the odd prison-like barred window. We could only guess what lay behind the impenetrable perimeter; but at least part of these buildings were being used as temporary workshops. As we rounded the corner at the top to approach our estate, we would get a glimpse of the work going on inside. In essence, they were digging a huge hole. *That must be an underground car park*, I thought.

Our dealings with Virgilio meant that I would stop by his workshop from time to time. This was located on one side of the building site that was supposed to be turning into the wonderful commercial centre. I was passing by, musing about the morning's news that North Korea had carried out a nuclear test. As I came upon Virgilio's place of work, I wondered how much longer the piece of land it backed onto would continue to resemble a bombsite. My inquiry with Virgilio's men revealed that the builders had run into problems with planning permission.

Shortly after that, Sue started including walks up the mountain in her exercise regime. The view from above clearly revealed the sorry state of affairs. Work had come to a complete halt. On top of that, the way the site was marked out indicated the plan to build a lot of small units, which didn't add up to what we had hoped for. The final blow to our hopes was a sign that appeared shortly afterward: 'New homes from 159,995 euros'.

The third and final phase of our alterations was the conversion of half the courtyard into a thirteen square foot dining area, effectively extending the original lounge area of the same size and shape. The result was to be a well-proportioned central living space overlooking the planted courtyard on one side and the rear terrace on the other. By adding a partition wall at the back of the new room, we turned the study, bathroom, and new bedroom into a self-contained suite that would serve as a necessary bolt hole for when we were acting as hosts to holiday-making family and friends. One has to appreciate that part of the benefit of any holiday is the mental escape. Ideally one enters a different world, where all the normal concerns cease to exist. In this fantasy realm, the daily cares that normally burden us can be simply cast aside. This is especially evident when driving around the busier parts of any resort. To the wandering tourists, the whole place is just one large pedestrian precinct, and the presence of motor vehicles, which could possibly be a hazard, is a threat to which they become completely oblivious. It's particularly hard for the holiday mind to appreciate the fact that one's host still needs to earn a living, and is not permanently on holiday themselves. Having the study in a well-separated area of the house then serves the purpose of allowing working activity to continue, while our visitors can enjoy their holiday without worrying that they may be a nuisance or hindrance to us in the pursuit of our normal working lives.

CHAPTER 5

The More Things Change, the More They Stay the Same

HAVING SETTLED INTO OUR new home, it was time for Sue to find work. To our surprise and delight, she was soon employed in the timeshare resort Jardines Playa a few minutes' drive down the hill and on to the coast. Her new job involved booking people in to the resort and arranging their stays in other timeshare resorts around the globe.

We were already very familiar with timeshare as a product, our first presentation having been back in Romsey, England, six years previously. We came away unscathed and with a carrier bag full of six bottles of very acceptable Bulgarian wine, which in those days was new to our English palates. Nevertheless, I must admit that the skilful presentation had me convinced, and if I'd had a bit more money to spend, I would have come away the proud owner of a week's timeshare on a canal boat somewhere in the middle of England.

Following that first experience we were to attend three further presentations over the next two years. 'You must have been bored or a sucker for punishment!' we were told, but no, the continuing attraction for us was the offer of free holidays in Cornwall, Spain, and, finally, Madeira. In the end we became quite expert at working the system. We would turn up, undergo the usual patter, turn down the timeshare, and walk off with our next free holiday.

Our ultimate free vacation coincided with my redundancy. Just a fortnight after I was informed of the bank's decision to 'let me go', we found ourselves with both children, now nineteen and sixteen, flying off to the sunny island of Madeira, whose name is taken from *Madera*, the Spanish word for wood. The woods were all chopped down centuries ago, and now banana plantations grow in their place, yielding three bountiful crops every year.

Our destination was an incredibly smart five-star hotel paradise, where we were delighted to be ushered into a spacious suite of beautifully furnished lounge/diner and well-equipped kitchenette, with twin suites of double bedroom and luxurious marble bathroom on either side. Our joy was increased further by the presence of another family, who had coincidentally booked their holiday to overlap ours by four days, and whose daughter Megan was best friends with Ali at school.

Each evening we would meet together in the piano bar and partake of cocktails, each one decorated with more than just the customary slice of fruit. The garnish was a work of art in itself, the fruit being carved and assembled artistically into exotic sculptures of swans, butterflies, and other colourful creatures. Tinkling on the ivories in the background was the celebrated composer of the Birdie Song. These daily drinks were delicious, and it was lovely to be able to share the moment with our friends, who turned out to be just as charming as their daughter, whose delightful company we'd enjoyed many times over several years. The most delicious moment of all came when we had the opportunity to disclose the 100 per cent discount we were enjoying. Our friends had paid the full going rate!

The only downside to these free breaks was the accompanying duty to attend yet another pointless presentation. The time before Madeira, we had been able to declare upfront our flint-like determination to resist any pressure to purchase. The salesman accepted our honest declaration graciously, and we spent the remainder of the time very pleasantly swapping notes about the places we had enjoyed on past holidays. This time, however, could not have been more different. Our salesman was the perfect caricature of timeshare tout: slicked-back, dyed black hair, smart suit, and gold rings and bracelets in abundance. This smarmy character's opening monologue lasted two hours to the minute. When my turn finally came to speak, I suppose I should have attempted to respond with a bit of subtlety. I think, in my defence, I was feeling a bit impatient after having to endure the man's futile banter for 120 long minutes. So, as I told him of my recent redundancy, it was with the air of a triumphant whist player laying down the ace of trumps to win the final decisive trick.

His reaction was utter incredulity. He laughed at me and suggested I try to come up with a more original excuse! Well, of course, my reaction in turn obviously revealed the authenticity of my very good reason for avoiding unnecessary expenditure, and he quickly apologised.

Although this had already been by far the most ridiculous sales effort we'd faced to date, the strangest part of our encounter was still to come. Sue was wondering, as many people do on holiday, where there might be a good Chinese restaurant. Our accommodation was free, but meals in the hotel were prohibitively expensive. Her inquiry was met with an extraordinary response, 'I would never eat in one of those restaurants. Have you ever seen a Chinese funeral?' The clear implication was that our oriental cousins go rather further than serving up the proverbial stray cats and dogs!

The funny thing was that Sue had even arranged and attended a small number of Chinese funerals in her capacity as manager of a woodland burial ground, the job she reluctantly left when we moved. It had been an interesting experience, which she related happily, right down to the symbolic burning of money on those unusual occasions.

Our salesman then lost all the credibility that he might have had with us as he stuck to his guns, quite seriously wanting to press home his twisted opinion. 'Well, I'll bet you haven't seen very many!'

'Well of course I hadn't. What a ridiculous thing to say!' Sue later reflected as we recovered from the peculiar presentation.

With all this exposure to timeshare, we came to the conclusion that it was basically a good product that suits many people, despite its tarnished reputation. The only drawback to Sue's new job was the boss, who appeared to come from that very hot place in the bowels of the earth (and I don't mean the local volcanic Timanfaya National Park!).

One of the common contributors to job stress is the fact that so many people are required to do a job without adequate training. Needless to say, this was a factor in Sue's early working experience. Sid had insisted that nobody else should train her. According to him, none of her colleagues followed the correct procedures, which disqualified them immediately as trainers. The only problem was, the boss never had time to give to the task, and the office manager, Evelyn, seemed to be in a constant state of confusion herself.

To add to the pressure, Sid turned out to be utterly intolerant of any little mistake. Really there should have been a warning notice up in the unhappy office, like those posted in car parks, 'work here at your own risk'. Sid's philosophy was simple: errors committed by his unfortunate staff cost him money, so they should pay for them. Consequently, each person was obliged to contribute five euros a week to 'the kitty' to ensure Sid's pocket suffered no injury, while the perpetrator suffered the embarrassment of being named, shamed, and collectively blamed!

Now, being the most recent arrival, it fell to Sue to cover the unpopular Saturday slot; Evelyn herself would be the last to make a weekend appearance. So Sue was astonished to behold her immediate boss walking through the office door one Saturday morning. Perhaps she had mistaken the day in her muddled mind. On the contrary, her purpose soon became clear. Furtively, and not realising Sue could hear every word, she went about covering up her latest mistake. A quick phone call to an airline to change a customer's holiday details at her own expense, and she was gone.

* * * * *

The all-knowing weather girl, Vicky, on the local Canarian TV is very precise about the start of the seasons. On the twenty-second of September, we were informed that autumn was to start at 4.45 p.m. The change of season was almost imperceptible, the first day being marked by a gentle northwest drift, lots of warm sunshine, and a maximum temperature of twenty-nine degrees. The wonderful weather continued as the next lot of visitors made ready to fly in. The problem was that the new, beautifully tiled floor of our recently added dining quarters had not yet materialised. Thankfully, the multitalented Ben came to the rescue, laying the carefully chosen ceramic with consummate precision and timing, with Nicky and Tony's arrival scheduled for the very next day.

Nicky is definitely my sister. Not that there was ever any doubt! What I mean is that physically and temperamentally we bear a marked family likeness. Now that we've got to the age where we're starting to wear out physically, it's also quite useful for me. Being four years ahead of me, she is able to advise on forthcoming niggles in different parts and how to overcome them.

Her husband, Tony, is extremely fit in the traditional sense of the word. He runs, rows, and cycles hundreds of miles a week, and his low pulse of around forty beats a minute bears witness to many years of rigorous training. This means that their stays with us afford me a valuable opportunity to go out with Tony before breakfast every morning and jog gently for half an hour along the pretty and varied promenade that runs along our local seafront. Every year I'm reminded of the privilege I have; it's such an ideal place to live and to exercise. We pass golden beaches, green palm trees, and colourful gardens, trot through the harbour, and pass the long row of restaurants, bars, and shops, all the while with an incredible view over the clear Atlantic waters toward the nearby islands with their foreshore of white sandy beaches and dark volcanic backdrop.

One evening I was talking to Nicky about our family likenesses. She had been researching our family tree for some years and was eager to show me the fruits of her labour. Her fascination with the subject was clearly beyond my own moderate level of interest. Nevertheless I had to agree that it was affirming to find characters in our lineage who were just like us. For me, the most interesting was our Great Uncle Leslie, who had been well known in his field of study, the Spanish language and literature. He was also quite an eccentric, to the point of having kept a monkey for a pet.

Nicky resisted the idea that she or even he might be labelled eccentric. 'It was quite common to keep monkeys as pets in those days', she asserted.

Nevertheless, we did hit on one idiosyncrasy common to us both, as she articulated a tendency I had often wondered at in myself: 'I never do one thing the same way twice'.

As she showed me the family tree she had assembled on the *Genes Reunited* website, we examined the relationships surrounding our mother's branch. I was struck by the repetition of names amongst siblings from the same marriage. It had been common for children to die soon after birth in those days and for their next sibling to take on the same name. So our mother's mother, Amy Quayle, bore the same name as her earlier sister. After half an hour delving into Amy's ancestors, I realised why Nicky had been up to three in the morning investigating the family line. I decided to make an escape before I got sucked into a similar whirlpool of time.

'Everybody's got a proper mixture of types in their ancestry', I commented, trying to sound more interested than I really was. 'There's always aristocracy and criminals in there somewhere!'

'Not in this lot', Nicky refuted. 'They're all humble working people: house servants and the like'.

I think at that point, any spark of curiosity died. As Sue came in from her evening out at the church's ladies' Bible study, I took the opportunity to sneak off to bed.

While we had been entertaining our family, Paul had been back in England enjoying his family's hospitality, or so we had thought. So we were somewhat surprised to hear from him. It transpired that his family relationships still needed a good deal of healing consequent to his period of alcoholism. There had been nobody to welcome Paul back to England, and he had spent a week living at the airport, rather like Tom Hanks's character in *The Terminal*, a film that had been released just two years previously, and which we had recently watched with Mark and Julie.

*　　*　　*　　*　　*

Meanwhile, more neighbours had been busy finishing their homes to their own requirements. As I was following the grower's advice to plant my newly purchased palm tree at the first new moon that November, I was collared by Carmen from two doors down.

Either she is younger than she looks or her husband, Alex, is older than he looks, or there are twenty years between them. Anyway, whatever her age, her friendliness and animation were as uncomfortable as they were endearing. She reminded me of some excited queen unveiling her plans for a royal palace with its summer and winter quarters. My mind reeled at the scale of it all.

My next visit was across the road to Angel (pronounced an-hell), who had done the plumbing in all our homes. He, like us, had kept part of the courtyard in order to allow ventilation and light into the heart of the home. The only difference was that the remaining space was much narrower than ours, meaning that the bias was towards the entrance of air rather than sun. In general, I was learning, the Spanish are not as enamoured with the sunshine as we Brits. They treat the darkened interiors of their homes as refuges from the harsh rays.

Naturally, being in a water-related trade, our *fontanero* friend, Angel, had made the most of his swimming pool area, having the pool itself tiled in sparkling variations of marine blue and green, with fancy handrails and even an outside changing room, equipped with its own shower. As he proudly showed it off, he also explained to me a curious phenomenon that I had been pondering. When it had been his turn to enter the partly built houses in order to lay the pipes, he had found it impossible to penetrate the dense forest of acrow props supporting the large flat roofs from inside. Consequently, he had been compelled to divert the pipe work that conducted the hot water from its source in the kitchen *solana*, all the way round the outside of the house, to the bathroom at the front. Now I knew why we had to wait so long for the water to get hot every time we used our bathroom!

I couldn't imagine how any of the other neighbours could possibly beat Carmen in the extensiveness of their alterations, until I ventured down the street one door farther and called on Jimmy one evening. Like most expats, Jimmy is quite a character. To say he is *the* most talkative character we've met so far would probably be inaccurate. The island is full of them. Perhaps what distinguishes him is the speed with which he chatters on, and the way he always has some extraordinary story to tell about our estate, the latest developments in the life of the community, and the struggles we were having with the developer to get various problems with our houses fixed.

We would see him regularly on the marina, where he owned the franchise on the Brisa's snack bar. This is an excellent place to hang out, enjoy the marina's special atmosphere, and snaffle up a bit of pizza, a burger or my favourite—the house special Brisa's sandwich. This feast of prawns, fruit, and salad enclosed between two lightly toasted slices of white bread is completed by a pile of freshly prepared chips. The cocktail of flavours lingers especially well on the palate with the aid of a refreshingly cold glass of white wine.

Sue always needs something sweet to round off any good meal; but in truth, there's more to the Brisa experience than just the food. Over the water, there's the view of the man-made yachting harbour. To the other side, holidaymakers stroll past on the boardwalk, out for the evening and in search of a bite to eat. The last rays of the warm evening sun suffuse and complete the tranquil scene. All the same, I have to say that the gastronomic experience is incomplete until I have tasted one of Jimmy's speciality ice-cream sundaes. As well as satisfying our appetites with the best food on offer along that stretch of the waterfront, Jimmy would often discount the final bill or kindly offer us a free drink, thus making his establishment even more attractive, if that were possible. At the end of the meal, the stale bread rolls come out so that we can finish by feeding the fish that splash around in the water underneath the boardwalk.

As Jimmy showed me around his rebuilt abode, I couldn't help but wonder. There seemed to be no plan. Relying on his wife's family's building connections to provide cheap labour and materials, he had basically knocked down all the walls, one by one, extended out several feet, and rebuilt them. The finished product reminded me of a sort of square balloon. It was just as if some giant had blown in through the front door and expanded the dwelling evenly all around.

Externally, everything looks identical to the original building, even as far as the black volcanic stone cladding that distinguishes our houses, emphasising the clean square lines, and contrasting, like a dark rock face, against the snowy whiteness of the walls. The only difference is that Jimmy's house is scaled up by a third in every direction. At night the place looks like a mediaeval palace, with cone-shaped wall lights illuminating the imposing walls like torches on an ancient fortress. Well, they do say an Englishman's home is his castle!

*   *   *   *   *

As the autumn pressed on, and we were left to enjoy our newly completed home on our own, it was a delight to be able to settle in, as it became the refuge we had been missing since we had left behind our old house in England. The remarkable contrast was that, although life had changed radically in terms of our working habits, the place we live, the people we interact with, our ways of relaxing at home in the evening after a hard day's work had not.

Take our teatime routine as an example. You might imagine us sitting out on our terrace, surrounded by a white walled garden populated with leafy tropical vegetation and brightly coloured bougainvillaea and birds of paradise—something like in those *Living in the Sun* programmes on the telly. Well, forget that. Picture us instead enjoying a typically British TV dinner. The difference is that, rather than sitting with doors and windows tightly shut against the cold, damp air, we have patio doors open wide on two sides of a light and airy lounge/diner, with the two sets of equally light net curtains in sky blue and white to complement the door frames and walls, billowing in a refreshing breeze.

On each lap a tray of the same teatime fare that we might have had in our former life—roast chicken with assorted Mediterranean vegetables roasted succulently in olive oil, washed down on Saturday evenings with a refreshingly cold glass of *vino blanco*.

Of course, although the food and drink may appear identical to the British equivalents, its source is what distinguishes it from our old staples. Fresh meat is frighteningly expensive here, a fact made all the more telling by our diminished earning power. On the other hand, frozen chicken is highly affordable at less than three euros a bird. The vegetables one has to be careful with. It's like going back in time, when the supply and price of garden produce used to vary according to its season in the United Kingdom. So it is here that some days we might be asked to part with two euros for every kilo of *calabacines*, as they call the courgettes. However, the next time we pass the same cash desk with the same purchase, we may be subjected to the unpleasant surprise of a bill four times the size!

As for the wine, this is where our experience really counts. During our previous existence, we were well placed for the ferry ports. Poole lay forty-five minutes to the west of us, with its link to Cherbourg, the fastest ferry crossing in the Western Channel, while Portsmouth was a few minutes further in the other direction. Accordingly, we would be able to take advantage of the frequent offers of cheap weekend getaways and return laden with all our favourite French fancies and glowing with the satisfaction of beating the tax man's prohibitive mark-ups. Over the years we developed a keen nose for cheap wine in particular. Basically, we learned that, although cheap and cheerful don't necessarily come together, when it comes to wine, they usually do. Initially we were cautious here, but soon found that the supply, quality, and, most importantly, what the French call *le rapport qualité-prix*—the relationship of quality to price—are all broadly similar to those we encountered in the land of Carrefour and Camembert.

On the box will be playing a DVD of one of our favourite English-language TV series. We don't have satellite; it's deliberate to keep us from getting into the unhelpful habit of watching only British television! British television is, of course, reputed to be the best in the world. Spanish television is rubbish, so they say, not worth watching. It's all trashy gossip programmes. Well, in my humble opinion, and of course I may be biased by my love of all things Spanish, there are some kinds of Spanish television that are like Mr Kipling's cakes—exceedingly good.

I'm not referring to their news coverage; I wouldn't dare challenge our 'Aunty Beeb' over her claim to be the best informed and most objective on the whole planet. Although one has to admire the Spanish newsreaders' apparently innate ability to ad lib when a piece of newsreel comes up on the screen with no dialogue, or the camera cuts back to them when they're least expecting it.

Rather, I'm talking about their propensity for taking a single successful programme, which might occupy a prime time slot of forty minutes maximum on British television, and turning it into a whole evening's entertainment. The first such series to grab our attention in this way, was the *X Factor—El Factor X*. The show opens with something far too cheesy for a British audience. The theme song is performed by *everybody*: contestants, judges, compère—I think even the cleaners are there somewhere in the mêlée of wannabes crowding the stage!

Maybe I've developed my taste for, and appreciation of, cheese since I've been here, but for me, there's something quite refreshing about the amateurishness of it all—an antidote to the slick, streetwise, streamlined performances demanded by a somewhat-cynical Great British public. A return to innocence and naivety, perhaps, or an inspiring lack of self-consciousness.

Then they play the trump card, and this has to do with the great advantage that every Brit emigrating to Spain's sunny land will tell you, that after the sunshine and sangria, the most attractive feature of life in Spain is the way its culture continues to hold on to values whose loss we northern Europeans feel most keenly, namely those of the family. Yes, granny and gramps (the *abuelitos,* as they're affectionately named), mum and dad, uncles and aunties, cousins, as well as numerous brothers and sisters, are all likely to make an appearance alongside their beloved relative. The latter may not have the X factor, but they'll most surely have the F factor. If Granny's not in tears, then Mum will certainly be. And if Mum fails to weep, the contestant will be so choked he can hardly sing. So we can see how, for most of them, the support of the family is a huge advantage!

My favourite programme so far, though, has to be *Identity*. Now don't switch off here, stay with me. I know that in Britain this one occupies an undistinguished slot somewhere in the less popular daytime schedule. It's an interesting idea played out in a low key for the consumption of less demanding audiences who don't need frantic pace and razzmatazz to keep their interest. When the contestant has been introduced, the lights come up and the music plays as the camera scans a stage full of twelve *extraños*—strangers—each stood on a podium, dressed and posed according to, in varying degrees of relevance, their identity.

Every week two contestants, one after the other, put into play their intuition, memory, and powers of observation. The first two or three strangers are usually identified pretty easily. After that, a couple of friends and family members lend their own skills and abilities to the task. The key to the enjoyment of the Spanish version of the programme (a copy of an originally American hit show called *Identity* and hosted by Penn Jillette of Penn & Teller fame) is without doubt its flamboyant and personable presenter, Antonio Garrido, who makes the show go with a swing. It's fun TV, as we find ourselves being drawn into the competition and playing along. There's the additional advantage, of course, that it's easy to follow, despite the difficulty of keeping up with the language spoken at its normal, rapid-fire conversational speed.

One day at the beginning of October, the morning Spanish news informed us of the imminent appointment of Ban Ki-moon as secretary general of the United Nations along with the mounting tension over North Korea's nuclear testing. The contrast underlined with our own tranquil part of the world struck me as our day off lay before us, with a much-anticipated visit to the spa in the luxurious Costa Calero Hotel. A little while later, Sue and I were sitting in the vestibule, waiting to enjoy a soak paid for by a kind relative. We had just helped ourselves to a free cup of coffee when I thought I heard the couple sitting next to us talking French.

Being a keen linguist, I never like to miss an opportunity to speak the language. When our children were growing up, a favourite haunt for a family outing was Compton Acres gardens in Poole. Being a star attraction, the gardens drew a good number of foreign visitors. For me it was an opportunity to accost anyone speaking a familiar tongue and attempt to impress them with my grasp of their vernacular. At first my young offspring responded with embarrassment, which soon developed into attempts to restrain me. The resulting ruckus soon became a fun feature of these regular visits. Every time they spotted a foreigner they would call to each other excitedly, 'Quick, grab Dad! We've got to stop him!' A happy memory from our family days out.

Without my family to subdue me, I was now free to indulge myself. I soon discovered our companions were in fact Belgian, just here for a week's holiday. We exchanged notes of praise about the beautiful hotel, and they murmured their admiration and approval as I told them how we had had the privilege of living here for six months already. They joked about how bad the weather was in Belgium and England, reckoning they got the same rain and wind, just a little later.

It could be easy to get used to near nonstop sunshine, so it helps to have these regular reminders of the sorry state of the English climate, particularly as we talk to the friends and family we left behind. Sue had to frequently prompt me not to gloat. Not that I would forget otherwise—the low temperatures and regular soakings, that is. Every morning, as I gratefully munched on the fresh orange that now formed an indispensable part of breakfast, I took in the Spanish national TV news and weather. It's surprising how often the northwest corner of the mainland gets rain; but there's one thing that never amazes me: it's usually associated with a depression over the British Isles!

*　　*　　*　　*　　*

As November approached, one item of furniture was lacking in our home—a TV cabinet. Accordingly, I presented myself at IKEA, which was still new to the island, in order to collect the flat-packed piece of furniture with an unpronounceable Swedish name. Rather fittingly, the shop had become a bit of a 'home away from home'; we had frequented it so often since our taking up residence in Playa Blanca.

Since it was time for elevenses (it's totally in keeping with the culture to have elevenses in Spain; they call it *merienda*!), I decided to pause for a few minutes in the small cafeteria located opposite the checkouts, a few steps from the collection point and the lifts down to the underground car park. I approached the counter ready to trot out a well-rehearsed inquiry on a subject that I had been recently turning over in my mind.

It has to be said at this point that the staff in the shops here are not really used to paying much attention to their clients, especially the foreigners. This rather irritating tendency is reinforced when there are two assistants working on a counter together. For whatever reason, the two young ladies serving that morning obviously found the chance to chat about some other subject than the local gossip more appealing. They soon engaged with my query and happily gave me their opinion. As we Brits attempt to speak Spanish, what we are known for above all is our pathological use of *por favor* and *gracias*. We are so courteous! For us, of course, such a level of politeness is a virtue, but we run the danger of sounding extremely prim and prissy.

I had already debated the matter with my fellow compatriots on many occasions, invariably encountering a great reluctance to dispense with the two words that have been drummed into all of us since the time when we first learned to speak. So my inquiry was an attempt to resolve the issue once and for all. Having tossed it around between themselves for a few moments the conclusion was emphatic, 'If you want to be polite, sod them, be polite!' *Politeness with attitude, now that's an interesting concept*, I thought.

They seemed to be saying that the Spanish themselves were impolite. Nevertheless, they were capable of appreciating these little niceties; they were not completely ignorant! This seemed a little harsh on the natives to me. If they were suggesting a general lack of respect, that didn't quite square with some of the more pleasant experiences of their service.

As I continued my inquiries throughout the day, nobody else came up with such a committed response, until the evening when some kind visitors treated us to a meal out at the local pizzeria. La Bambola is located one row back from the seafront at Playa Flamingo and ranks high among our favourites. As well as serving tasty, well-cooked food, the waiting staff are particularly friendly. Cordial inquiries such as, 'You been here before? You having nice holiday?' are not so much a testimony to their bad memory as to the rarity of our attendance.

A further delight is to watch them interacting animatedly with the children that come in with their families from the surrounding holiday complexes. Both waiters are quite loud and jolly, particularly Mario, who, with his long black curly hair, reminds me a bit of David Essex in his looks. Although I've not heard him sing, it wouldn't surprise me if one evening he were to burst into a tune! In line with his bold character, he responded to my research with a characteristically forthright opinion, 'It's too much!' In his straightforward view of things, there was no need to beat about the bush; we Brits should take a leaf out of his book of boldness and simply state what we want.

The next Saturday, I had an urgent pastoral visit to make at Arrecife hospital. This happened to coincide with a compelling urge of Sue's to visit the smart Deiland shopping centre. Official visiting hours don't begin until 1 p.m., which meant that I was half an hour early. I'd been told that they were pretty relaxed about times at the hospital, and decided that if I looked confident enough and strode through reception fairly nonchalantly, I would be allowed to mount the stairs to the wards without being challenged. I was wrong!

This was the moment I had been dreading. I had been waiting some time since my ordination to receive my official credentials that I would have flashed on such an occasion. Despite several attempts to obtain them, they had still not been forthcoming. Thankfully, the receptionist was as gracious as she was alert; she accepted my story, and I was able to proceed.

Meanwhile, back in Deiland, Sue was enjoying the freedom of browsing the shops and taking in the weekend atmosphere. There was an interesting exhibition on the theme of fitness and well-being, the spa that we'd attended on a number of occasions being represented among the stands. Having greeted the diminutive Carmen, who had so often taken our membership number and issued our locker keys, she decided to pop into Body Shop. Here she was delighted to encounter the helpful assistant who had been serving there ever since we came to live here. Having given Sue lots of time, at the end she produced a surprise free gift, a lovely make-up bag. The girl didn't want any thanks, so as Sue expressed hers, her reply was, 'No. Thank *you* for buying!'

That just about sums it up, for the same reason the waiting staff in any good restaurant will thank the client when taking his or her order, presenting each dish, and again when the customer finally leaves.

CHAPTER 6

The Clouds, They Are a-Gathering

DURING THE COURSE OF my translation and interpretation business, I meet many interesting people. A couple of the most interesting of all were Michael and Deirdre, near neighbours from the next village. We had actually met them four months before they decided that they needed my services. One balmy July evening, we had found ourselves on the Rubicon Marina, strolling along the pretty paved alleyways and boardwalks past the tasteful arrangement of shops, bars, and restaurants that grace the man-made harbour.

Out on the water, the picturesque rows of millionaires' boats wait patiently for a visit from their absent owners. The tranquil scene is punctuated by the odd sailor or two going about their boating business, preparing for a voyage across the Atlantic maybe, or having just returned from a day's outing along the rugged coastline. Some, like our next-door neighbour Celina's cousin, even live there on one of the many floating potential homes.

On this occasion, it happened to be around teatime, and being a bit peckish, we impulsively decided to add ourselves to the large number of people who were already thronging to the local hostelries that look out across the scene of mainly empty sailing vessels. We rather liked the look of a smart Italian restaurant, but having seated ourselves the prices on the menu were not so appealing. Accordingly one pizza between the two of us was our order.

As we finished our modest meal and rose to leave, we got into conversation with a cheerful couple on the next table. They were a few years older than us, living in Las Breñas, a peaceful little village with a higher standard of housing, just up the road from Playa Blanca. We immediately hit it off, and even swapped business cards, suggesting we might meet up sometime and share a more ample meal at a better restaurant. Time slipped by, and with the general busyness of our lives, we didn't get round to calling Michael and Deirdre. However, since Sue was working full time, it used to fall to me to do the weekly supermarket shop, and I would occasionally bump into our acquaintances somewhere between the eggs and the fruit and veg section. I would always greet them cheerily and remember their names. Michael in particular was quite distinctive. His curly mop of grey hair, ruddy features, large frame, and lilting West Country accent reminded me very much of another Michael I knew back in England.

Then some time passed as Sue and I reversed our roles and she returned to the regular shopping run. Finally, I answered my cell phone one day early in November 2006 to hear Michael's unmistakable voice at the other end, 'I don't know where I got your card from', he said, 'but you're our last hope!'

My immediate thoughts were a nonplussed mixture of, *How could Michael have forgotten me?* and *What am I about to let myself in for?*

Of course, when I arrived at their house the following day, Michael instantly recognised me. My wounded pride was restored, at least, even if the sense of foreboding engendered by the 'last hope' bit lingered.

As we sat in Michael and Deirdre's spacious and well-equipped living room, the whole sorry story unfolded in all its stunning detail, with the aid of a string of still and moving images paraded skilfully across Michael's high-tech TV screen. It turned out that Michael and Deirdre had fallen victim to what can only be described as the 'neighbour from hell'. Two weeks previously our friends had been woken by the strong odour of sewage and the noise of digging in the fellow's garden. A quick look through the bathroom window confirmed their suspicions. For the second time in a year, a man was busy opening up the drains and blocking the outlet from their house with two large rocks covered in plastic and a generous helping of quick-drying cement! Since then, their waste had been backing up to the house, even filling the dishwasher and washing machine with their own sewage. You're probably wondering at this point why anybody would resort to such un-neighbourly action.

Anybody who's lived next door to a family with children will have experienced the ball over the wall/fence/hedge with varying degrees of frequency and sometimes even annoyance. As I pen these very lines, I'm reminded of a number of occasions I've been on both sides of the barrier dividing one property from the next. For several years, for example, my son and I used to play soccer regularly at the end of our hundred-and-some-odd-foot-long garden. The trunk of a mature apple tree and the corner of the tool shed formed the goalposts on the house side, while a clump of long grass that sprouted daffodils in the springtime paired with an old plastic garden chair marked the target at the other end.

The kick-off was taken from one end, standing in the goal with the other player standing at the regulation distance of five paces. Besides the apple tree that lent its trunk as a goalpost there was another halfway down the pitch. This one extended its branches across nearly the full width of the garden. My standard kick-off was to use the branches by flicking the ball into the air, so that it bounced around momentarily in the canopy of the tree and found its way, rather like a pinball, through the air and dive-bombed on to the little lad at the other end, finally glancing off him into the goal. Of course, the ball would usually miss the target and either fall to Jonna's feet or land behind him out of play. But it was worth it for the rare success.

The side-lines were conveniently provided by the hedges that bordered both sides of the peculiar pitch. One might think that it would be better to have more space, whereas in fact these natural barriers helped to keep the ball in play. If it was booted hard, it would become lodged in the branches and a throw-in would be awarded. If it was booted very hard, it would end up next door. Thankfully our neighbour was a genial family man and very tolerant of these invasions.

Michael and Deirdre's nightmare had started like that. A ball over the fence. Then another. Small incidents in themselves; but that's the way these neighbourly disputes often commence. They pretty soon got fed up, not only with having to return the object, but also because a glass was knocked over and broken. Their refusal to continue throwing back the missile was now met with hostility. Photographic evidence showed clearly a woman standing at their gate angrily brandishing a piece of wood, which was also produced by the disconsolate couple as they continued to explain their plight. Apparently that had also become a missile shortly after the photo had been taken.

The neighbour's animosity seemed to have begun a year previously with a blocked drain on his side. That shouldn't have had anything to do with Michael and Deirdre. However, the builder had taken an unfortunate shortcut. Instead of laying independent drains for the two houses, he had taken Michael and Deirdre's under the garden wall and simply joined it to next door's. The lamentable result was that, when the latter investigated the blockage, even though it was made up of piles of discarded nappies, they had an excuse to lay the blame at my friends' door. Their consequent demand for a contribution of seven hundred euros toward the cost of clearing the obstruction was rightly refused. Out of retaliation, the nasty neighbour had resorted to concreting up Michael and Deirdre's outflow.

By the time I became involved, they had already taken him to court over what was now the second drain-blocking incident. Unhappily, the solicitor they had engaged fitted perfectly the caricature of the fat cat, couldn't care less, money grabbing 'professional'. He had sat back in his big swivel chair in his plush office prognosticating in condescending tones to my friends, without paying due attention to their plea. The resultant trial had been a fiasco, of course. They had even found themselves on the back foot, being accused by the other party of some imaginary offence. My first task then was to accompany them to the courts to collect the judge's ruling. I had visited the courts a couple of times before; but their basic organisation still eluded me. After a couple of false starts however, I finally managed to locate the relevant office and we were able to collect the *sentencia*. The legal conclusion on this occasion turned out to be dismissive; neither party had been found guilty of any offence.

Unfortunately, this abortive first attempt at gaining justice made things more difficult. They now needed a more-than-decent lawyer to dig them out of a huge hole. I immediately got on the phone to my friend Sandy, an American who had lived in Lanzarote for many years, was fluent in a number of languages, and who knew his way around the legal system. Having got the number of a serious and efficient young legal representative and given him a quick call, I found to my delight that he was available very shortly at his offices in Calle Real.

Finding places in Arrecife isn't always straightforward. In fact, and appropriately enough for an island full of rabbits, to the uninitiated the town resembles a bit of a rabbit warren. Calle Real is really called Calle Castillo y Leon. It's just that everybody refers to it as Calle Real. So, having looked on the map and inquired at the desk, I made the connection between the two names for the first time. The street in question is a pedestrian zone, that stretches from the coast to the old harbour, thus skirting the old town. It's the part of Arrecife where you can find most of the solicitors' offices together with a host of banks, shops, cafés, and related businesses.

Thus began our quest for justice. Arnaldo the solicitor was as sympathetic as he was thorough. He quickly got on the case and sent legal letters to all the appropriate parties, dispatched experts to examine the scene of the crime, accompanying them to make sure everything was done correctly this time. The first attempt having resulted in dismal failure, he was doing all he could to put together a watertight case.

Another big problem was that in Spain the wheels of justice turn very slowly indeed. And no one else could help. The police had no power to go on to the neighbour's land without his permission. The *ayuntamiento*, that is, the local authority, couldn't help either. The public health department, for their part, showed a non-existent level of interest.

Christmas came as a welcome break that year! My abiding memory is of leaving their house, with Michael expressing his understandable frustrations in the background and Deirdre wishing me, 'Happy Christmas!' with streams of tears running down her face.

Our first Christmas back in England felt very strange. Having moved away nine months earlier and got used to our new home, the cold, grey skies came as a shock. It was as if I had forgotten what it was like to be in England. I found it nearly impossible to be at a comfortable temperature both inside and outside. In Lanzarote I had been wearing pretty much the same clothes wherever I was. Now I found myself having to put on piles of clothes to go out into the freezing cold, and then take off a couple of layers to go into the stiflingly hot shops.

*   *   *   *   *

When I came back from England and took up Michael and Deirdre's cause once again, Michael was on the warpath, determined to get the justice that had not been forthcoming to date. He poured his heart out in a long letter to the solicitor, who took offence and reacted with a letter of resignation. I couldn't bear to see my friends left completely defenceless in the middle of their nightmare ordeal, and thankfully my pleas with him to retract his withdrawal were heeded. It was then my pleasure to interpret at a happy meeting that cleared the air over a cup of coffee.

Thus we resumed our frequent visits to the solicitor in Arrecife. Navigating the maze of one-way streets, parking, and finding one's way out of the town is complicated. Thankfully, there is a spacious underground car park on the edge of the town, so it was relatively easy to park my vehicle, walk ten minutes to the solicitor's office, return the same way, and make a quick escape onto the dual carriageway. As time went on, I grew to appreciate the seafront in particular. Strolling along there from the car park to the commercial heart of the capital takes one past some interesting features along the Esplanade, including, on one corner, a little knot of open-air cafés where old men sit playing animated games of dominoes. The energy they throw into the contest is emitted in the loud clicking of tiles and boisterous commentary, as their peers gather around the tables to spectate—it's a serious sport! The path then widens out into a long straight portion, the scene of a very decent weekly market, lined with trees on one side and lapped by the waters of the Atlantic on the other. Brightly coloured bougainvillea and other climbing shrubs decorate the white stone pergolas down the middle of the strip. But the most interesting spectacle by far, and even more animated than the daily clash of dominoes used to be provided by a colony of egrets nesting in the tops of trees. These white seabirds reminded me rather of mini pelicans, and, as they clattered clumsily around the branches and squawked away, their comical character helping to create a fun, holiday seaside atmosphere.

This brings me to a saga that is as sad as it is outrageous. Suddenly these emblematic birds went missing. At first we didn't think anything of it. *Perhaps they have migrated,* I thought. It wasn't until I was watching the Lanzarote news on the local TV one lunchtime at the end of January that I learned of their horrific fate. As the item started, I immediately recognised the distinctive point on the prompter. Standing with a little team of people and looking very smug was the *alcalde,* the mayor of Arrecife. I nearly fell off the settee as he recounted the efforts that had been taken to rid the 'once peaceful precinct' of the ghastly *garsas.* Apparently, the campaign against our unfortunate feathered friends had been ongoing for quite some time. The *ayuntamiento,* or town hall, finally hit on the idea of chopping off half the branches that once served as perches and lining the rest with rows of upward pointing sharp metal spikes!

In the days and weeks that followed, we wondered where the colony might have taken up residence following their cruel eviction. We even spotted the odd forlorn-looking egret sitting in the middle of wasteland on our way to church. The last we heard, they had installed themselves above one of the town's most popular restaurants, to the utter dismay of the owners, their terrace having become quickly covered in bird lime. In fact, it was this sort of deposit left on the couple of otherwise-smart stone benches under the trees, which had been the excuse for rendering their former home uninhabitable. These benches were where the old people like to alight in the heat of the day and watch the world go by, it had been claimed. The irony is that, to this day, the newly sterile seats remain as empty as the sparse and spiky branches above!

As we drove home after our final meeting with the solicitor, we were anxious for a different reason. A fierce hurricane had landed on the island the November before, destroying the palm-studded lagoon that used to encompass and embellish our local beach. The changing climate meant we should expect more of the same, and Michael and I had both received phone calls from friends warning us of an imminent blast.

Now, a habit of mine, which has become a fascination over the years, to the point of near obsession—and my family will all testify to this—is my need to see the weather forecast every day, I just have to know the state of the atmosphere around me and how it is likely to develop over the next day or two. In England, where our fickle weather patterns are a deservingly frequent topic of conversation, this is understandable. Here, where you can predict the temperature, wind direction, and sunshine hours by the date with 90 per cent accuracy, I have to admit it to be less so. I just like to have the assurance, and sometimes even here the weather can be a problem.

The most uncomfortable variation is a phenomenon the Spanish call *calima*. For a few days every other summer, when the wind turns to the east, bringing with it a sandy red dust from the Sahara, and the temperature suddenly increases from a comfortable 29 to a blistering 43° Celsius (109° Fahrenheit).

Having endured the gnawing cold and troublesome rain for more than forty years, the warm sunshine was for me a welcome respite; so I vowed never to complain. When it goes above forty, I just thank God for air conditioning and avoid the outside for those few days.

A hurricane, however, was a different matter. Nonetheless, I was surprised at the stories ringing in our ears of *ferreterías* (ironmongers) being besieged by the local inhabitants snapping up large sheets of wood and vast quantities of nails to secure their homes against the approaching storm. We hurried back, hoping to beat the high winds approaching Playa Blanca and get home in time to batten down the hatches. While I put my foot down and fixed my attention on the road, both my passengers were fearfully examining the gathering clouds.

Arriving home, I burst through the front door and reached breathlessly for the remote, so I could review the latest Canarian news stored on my DVD recorder. Frantically fast-forwarding to the weather, I watched intently as Vicky Palma predicted the possibility of the odd shower, some of which may turn out *tormentosa* (heavy). Where was the hurricane? All I could think of was that some English speaker had heard the word *tormentosa* and misunderstood it; their fearful interpretation then spread as quickly through the British community as a hurricane itself.

* * * * *

Having dealt with my friends' drain problems, it was now my turn; I had to deal with some difficult issues with our own builder. When our house became ready for occupation, we were given a guided tour by the architect, to check that everything was to our satisfaction. It was indeed all pristine and beautiful, and I lavished praise on him for his excellent design. The water in the swimming pool was just a bit low. He made some excuse. *Oh well,* I thought. *It's all under a ten-year guarantee, so I'm sure there'll be no problem in fixing any leaks.* A little while later I presented my list of snags to the builder's agent. No response.

In fact, there was no response for six months despite regular protests, and it slowly became apparent to all of us on the estate that the builder needed some sharp persuasion in order to come and correct a long list of faults. Thankfully, our only major problem was the pool; other people were really struggling with warped doors, sinking floors, and rising damp. A triumvirate of close neighbours eventually got together to spearhead some concerted legal action. Cristóbal, together with the policeman living opposite him, and Angelo the Italian, organised a solicitor to take charge of our case. Soon a technical architect was dispatched to do the rounds, listing the various defects and busily gathering evidence with his digital camera. We signed the letters, paid our 186 euros each, and waited.

Not a whisper. We were brazenly ignored. Our three leaders urged us to take the next step and join them in taking the rascals to court. I declined. According to our sources, it was common practice for builders to go bust, especially when faced with legal claims. Apparently these cowboys are free to start one building business after another, make a mint, go bust, and start all over again.

Meanwhile, Dick, who was doing a lot of work building pools, and his mate Paul, who was part of the same business, kindly conducted tests on the pipe work. The fabric of the pool itself appeared solid, causing suspicion to fall on the plastic tubing that conducted the water through the pump and filter, and back into the leaky pit. These tests were inconclusive, and as the months passed, we gradually got used to the idea that we would have to spend out on a radical solution to the problem. Two lots of British neighbours had already opted to get their pools fibreglassed. The results were watertight and pleasing to the eye. Finally, we fell in line and instantly became twenty-five hundred euros poorer.

It was just another example of the typical kind of unexpected expense one incurs when moving here.

Things at church were going rather more smoothly. Having settled in well, I was enjoying working with Mark, and we were finding the midweek meetings well attended and inspiring, along with our Sunday morning worship.

We were particularly encouraged by the promises we kept finding in the Bible about God answering prayer. As we asked him for healing—in particular, praying for a number of friends, acquaintances, and family members—we saw one answer after another.

I was on my way home from such a meeting late one evening when I discovered another dangerous beast that complicates the driving experience on the otherwise tranquil roads of our *trozo de roca:* the 'dozy tourist'. The most dangerous tendency of this peculiar animal is the making of unexpected manoeuvres of any kind of which the car under their control is physically capable: stopping, starting, turning, reversing, or simply causing havoc by heading in the opposite direction to the regular traffic.

I had already had a few experiences of eccentric behaviour of such kind. A number of indicators combined to signal extreme caution on such occasions. For a start, there is the rental sticker on the back of the vehicle, proclaiming the name of the rental company, such as 'Payless' or 'Pluscar'. It's always to the left of the boot handle like a warning sign, 'beware of the driver'. It's also obvious when the driver is distracted, as they wander slowly along, often wavering from side to side and even crossing the white borderlines that mark out either side of the lane. The new road that takes us home from Yaiza is the stretch they choose to cause the greatest danger and consternation. Their most irritating habit is to stop suddenly and obstruct the freeway with the sole purpose of adding yet another snapshot to their burgeoning collection of holiday pictures.

This time, I was enjoying the freedom of the empty road that rings the compact town from which our borough of Yaiza derives its name, driving along and savouring the success of the evening's proceedings, when I instinctively detected that something strange was about to happen. The offender stopped suddenly in front of me, reversed into the kerb, turned to cross my path, reversed away from me, and then proceeded to boldly pass me in the opposite direction. A three-point turn on the fastest stretch of single carriageway on the island, which I greeted with an energetic application of one hand to the horn and the other to the flasher. I still can't quite believe it!

*　　*　　*　　*　　*

Meanwhile, Paula's relief from life-threatening disease had been brief. Things were not looking good. Each time the disease returned, it came back with greater fury. The only thing that could save her now would be a bone-marrow transplant.

The appeals went out, and those of us younger than fifty were all urged to submit ourselves for testing. Our church was blessed with the presence of a number of entertainers at that time, and we used to put on a brilliant Christmas show every year. Gerie Barber, who was one of our number and one of the best known, would appeal to her audiences to pray for Paula and promote the bone-marrow donor register, as she dedicated Celine Dion's "I'm Alive" to her.

As the medics scoured their records for a match, it was a challenge to stay optimistic as the chances of finding the exact match needed were pronounced as close to zero. In short, a match would be a near miracle. In the end, three matches were found! Obviously, one would have been enough, but three? We were greatly encouraged that our prayers would continue to be answered. At the beginning of March, as Paula was admitted to hospital in Madrid for the transplant procedure, her prospects of surviving the predicted six-week stay improved to 50-50.

A couple of weeks after the completion of the procedure, we made Paula's presence in our favourite city an excuse to enjoy a short break there. It was a big shock to see her laid up in bed and having lost several stone in weight. The energy stored in those pounds she may have once regarded as excess baggage, was now essential to keeping her alive. Her complexion was a healthy-looking, glowing pink. Nevertheless, as appearances are wont to be, this was completely deceiving; it simply betrayed the presence of the disease that accompanies this type of transplant. A kind of rejection in reverse, the foreign bone-marrow 'graft', while hopefully saving the recipient's life, also attacks the 'host'. Graft-versus-host disease is capable of completely undoing the benefit of the transplant and even bringing death itself.

Having had a good experience at the Teguise Sunday market, on the Sunday morning of our visit, I allowed Sue to persuade me to finally take the plunge into the mêlée known as the Rastro in Madrid. According to the bumf, 'tourists and locals alike flock to this open-air market, where the smart shopper can find some of the best bargains in the city'. I figured that if we used the same tactic that had worked so well in Lanzarote, we could hit the stalls early, before the crowds arrived.

I soon learned my mistake. Some cynic commented on the Internet that, since all the shops are closed, there's nothing else for people to do! It certainly seemed like the whole city had descended on the area. Maybe I'm just not a 'smart shopper'; the only thing I managed to do smartly was take a right turn and spill out of the seething mass of people into a quiet side street at the earliest opportunity. By that time, Sue was astonishingly equally ready to bail out.

Two separate attempts had been made to rob us in the few minutes that we spent being buffeted along the street in the human torrent. I'm always on my guard against pickpockets in busy public places; so when somebody started to slap me vigorously on the back, I was not taken in for even a nanosecond by their pretence at having accidentally set light to my jacket! Holding tightly to my bum bag, I shrugged the man off while attempting to calm my poor wife, who was very upset by the whole drama. The incident left a bitter memory; I can still recall quite vividly the man's shaved head, sallow looks, and shabby denim clothing. The final straw followed swiftly. As Sue went to take a coin from the bag fastened around her waist, she found another hand already in there. Wresting the pouch quickly from the intruding member, she discovered that the thief had already unfastened it.

On returning home and following Paula's recovery, we received news of one life-threatening infection after another, and the six weeks turned into months.

Next it was our pastor's turn to be added to the sick list. He was playing squash one day when a loud cracking sound heralded the rupture of the Achilles tendon in his right heel. Despite the surgeon's pronouncement that a simple operation would put things back together, Mark's recovery was dogged with difficulties, just as Paula's was. The problems all sprang from the failure of the wound to heal. Again, Mark faced the same issue that Paula had faced with her sickness; the prohibitive cost of adequate social security meant that he was without income. The pressure to return to work resulted in his hobbling around on crutches while carrying on his trade of sign writing. Finally, one day, he stumbled down the steps of a printing shop and set his recovery back to zero.

The result was that he had to withdraw completely from the work of the church and spend his days immobilised with his foot up. Consequently I found myself as acting pastor. In reality, this was a good learning period for me; doing the work and having Mark to turn to for support was a gentle way of breaking me in to the responsibilities of leadership.

Fishermen passing the time of day on the old harbour in Arrecife

*The long bar that runs along one side of the restaurant
at the Castillo de San Jose in Arrecife*

The Charco old harbour in Arrecife

We came across this hunting dog, which looked very lost in the middle of Teguise, the former capital in the center of the island

This picture illustrates the genius of Cesar Manrique, and can be seen at Jameos del Agua in the north of Lanzarote

Every Christmas this nativity scene is reconstructed in the pretty town of Yaiza. Essentially a model of the island with a crib scene at the heart

Another of Cesar Manrique's creations, the cactus gardens show off the amazing variety of this indigenous plant

The island regularly plays host to the World Windsurfing Championships

Chapter 7

Hitting the Wall

For a while now, we had been spending more than we bargained for, and the financial pressure was beginning to grow. Most of my working efforts outside the church had been focused on Michael and Deirdre, who were running up a big bill.

'I know this is all costing me the earth', Michael commented as he e-mailed me his latest translation request. This time it was a notice to the neighbours explaining the reason for the growing pool of stinking wastewater in his front garden, and appealing for their support. Although on the surface Michael seemed happy to pay, I was uneasy. It had been a couple of months since I had presented my last account, and not being the most efficient in the sphere of administration, I wasn't finding time to get down to produce an up-to-date bill. On top of that,

I hadn't yet published my scale of charges—something highlighted to me by a more businesslike friend. Finally I presented a bill with the scale of charges attached. I was a bit concerned about the total; but I thought, 'Well, they have given me a lot of work, so I don't mind if they beat me down a bit'.

I hadn't anticipated Michael's reaction. With all the pressure they were under, my billet doux was the last straw. I received a very angry mail in which he refused to pay even one cent. My worst fear had come true! I felt devastated, angry with myself, and thoroughly dejected. I was very sorry for 'poor old me'; all I had done was try to help!

It so happened that at that time, the church was fasting and praying. The focus of our action was of course our ailing pastor and Paula's faltering health as her hospitalisation continued. The unexpected spin-off for me that I was suddenly convicted of my insensitivity in the way I had presented my recent financial demands to my suffering clients. There may even have been a touch of greed riding on the back of the financial insecurity I was currently feeling!

I put away my anger and ate a good portion of humble pie, asking for their forgiveness and whether they'd consider paying me half the amount I had requested. Thankfully, the biblical proverb was fulfilled: 'A soft reply turns away anger'. Michael paid me substantially more than the half I had requested. The reconciliation was still incomplete, however. My services were no longer required, and to this day I have to admit with some sadness that I don't know how the couple's drain problems were resolved.

*   *   *   *   *

By April of that year, with all the challenges, including Sue's mounting unhappiness at work, we were ready for a holiday. The positive side of Sue's employment was that she was able to call on her boss's expert opinion for a choice of destination, and receive a welcome discount to boot.

We could afford four nights at the Costa Canaria, a beautiful hotel in Gran Canaria, which lies a forty-minute flight westward and slightly south of us. Living on the islands takes away the urgency one might otherwise feel to get out and 'do' the island. We can easily do that another time! So our consciences were at ease, and we were free to simply relax and enjoy to the maximum the many facilities on offer.

On a short stay, the priority is to recharge the batteries from the moment of arrival. All-inclusive for us means lying in the sun, catching up on some relaxed reading, joining in the games, and enjoying the extraordinary range and quantity of food laid out at every mealtime. My holiday reading is normally purchased from a local shop that bears the sign *International Press*. In Gran Canaria, with its many German visitors, there is a plentiful supply of German-language newspapers. On our third day I was delighted to spot the Austrian *Kronenzeitung*, an eye-catching daily paper in mini-tabloid format, brimming with interesting articles on events and trends the world over.

On this occasion my eye was caught by the headline 'Job Loss Fears Mean Shorter Holidays'. Turning to page eleven, I learned that miserly bosses are more and more limiting their employees to short breaks away from their work, in a bid to save on the cost of engaging temporary cover. According to psychologist Herr Doktor Gerhard Klicka, this is a short-sighted policy. Workers need a minimum fortnight to relax. Shorter holidays can only increase sickness rates and end up costing the employer more. The good doctor explained that we all need time to adjust to our holiday surroundings and simply switch off.

Well, I was on a four-night break, with three and a bit days to unwind! I consoled myself philosophically that I had made the best choice by holidaying in the familiar surroundings of sunshine, palm trees, and Spanish, and switching immediately into holiday mode by speedily unpacking and launching straight into a large buffet lunch!

In fact, the all-inclusive hotel is a whole world of its own, the complete getaway in itself. We soon learned to escape into it, not feeling the need to stray too far or often beyond the bounds of our hotel's glorious grounds.

This hotel is endowed with lovely gardens that lead gently down to the back gate, past which runs the promenade. It's all beautifully landscaped with bending palms, brightly flowering hibiscus hedges, and an inviting swimming pool located centrally. The sunbeds are arranged around the pool just as one would expect; however, a quick scan of the beds reveals something missing—towels! In this quiet corner of Gran Canaria, despite the presence of a large number of Germans, the early morning towel run has been eliminated. Instead, the hotel has instigated a regime of colour-coded labelling. Guests simply write their name on the label and the sunbed is theirs for the full length of their stay. In one corner stands a little café where drinks and ice creams can be ordered for free all day long. When dinner is served, it's a few steps away to another side of the garden and up to the terraced part of the dining room, with its typically Canarian canopy and pleasing outlook over the surrounding planting.

As for the food, this should really carry a health warning. Confronted with such a wide choice and abundant supply, it is all too easy to make the same mistake we did. We would quickly fill ourselves up and still feel we hadn't made the most of it! The greatest temptation is the 'show cooking'. The splendid sight of the chef practising his appetising art, the sound and aromas exuding from a griddle full of juicy steaks, really get the juices going. And then, when he produces a pile of freshly made chips next to them, the whole thing becomes irresistible. All that lacks is the necessary vegetable to finish the dish and provide the appropriate complement of colour, flavour, and texture. After a while, we realised that the way to approach it is to try a little of the things that take our fancy before deciding what will be our main dish. The only problem is that by the time we'd finished trying things, we'd already had a whole meal! Oh well, it was a good job we hadn't been able to afford a longer stay!

Apart from the food itself, the greatest source of conversation at the table is the people around us. We are always on the lookout for the fattest person, the whitest and the reddest. On one occasion I remember one person embodying all three!

This time we encountered a crop of some very unusual-looking people, probably because it was out of season. One unsuspecting man we christened 'the pole', due both to his nationality and his resemblance to a thin, vertical rod. The main debate this particular week was the difference in age between the lady I christened 'the cradle snatcher' and her partner. The former was an English-looking woman, not unattractive for her age with her long flowing auburn locks, while the young man she accompanied was a typically Spanish-looking clean-cut type.

Having made the most of dinner, the first event in the evening is the mini disco. Just before their bedtime, the little ones are called to the dance floor to burn off their last few calories of surplus energy before being dispatched suitably exhausted to their rooms for the night. The wonderful variety of sizes, nationalities, dress, and behaviour of the children makes for a fascinating show as they congregate on the stage. The main group lines up on the stage facing us, while two members of the entertainment or 'animation' team conduct the proceedings.

While most attempt to copy their leaders' animated singing and accompanying movements, a few just stand there looking a bit lost and sucking their little thumbs. Others wander around doing their own thing and observing what the rest of the kids are up to. Some of the 'animation' team are distinctly more animated than others. Attila the Hungarian looks a bit out of place but makes a game effort. Meanwhile, I start reflecting on the evolution of this extraordinary human activity and wonder how many generations have been singing 'Head, Shoulders, Knees, and Toes'. When it comes to turning around and jumping in the air, a third turn one way, another third turn the other, while the rest stand looking on, completely bemused!

As they sing in Spanish, English, and German, it strikes me afresh how strange it is that even the animals make different sounds according to their language. How on earth does the English 'woof' translate to *guau* in Spanish? And why does a German donkey say *iaah iaah*? Sue's favourites are the little girls in their party dresses, and she loves to watch the doting parents record the whole performance on their video cameras. I wonder who is going to be made to sit through all those hours of recordings.

The greatest and funniest contrast came at the end of one show. As the most meritorious were called up to the stage to receive certificates for their achievements during the day, it became the turn of a half pint called Justin to be summoned. Judging by his size, he must have been about five. The little scrap was so overcome with stage fright that his brother, a somewhat larger and more confident version of Justin, sporting the same crop of Germanic-looking platinum-blond hair, had to lift his rigid sibling from the spot where he stood rooted and carry him like a trophy across the dance floor. 'Justin Senior' took his place matter-of-factly in a line of winners waiting on the podium. Meanwhile, his prize-winning passenger kept his face completely covered with both hands the whole time. As the animation girl posted the paper deftly in the slot between hands and face, a ripple of laughter ran through the admiring assembly of adults.

Two names later down the list of winners, the girl pronounced the name 'Nieves'. About half Justin's age, this one needed no encouragement to bounce up eagerly and receive her paper proudly. Finally, all the winners were invited to hold up their prizes for the proud mums and dads, grannies and grandpas. Nieves pulled herself up to her full three feet, adding nearly another six inches by teetering on the tips of her toes in an effort to try to raise her token of excellence as high as she possibly could. 'She's so sweet!' Sue said. 'I could almost eat her'.

True, the cute frills of her creamy white party dress, matched by her cherub looks and upward-gazing wide brown eyes, and completed by a bob of typically Spanish curly brown hair, made the little darling a sight for sore eyes!

It had been good to 'get away from it all' even for a short time. I was discovering that my new vocation came with a constant burden of pastoral concern for those in my care. The complete change of scenery had done Sue and me a world of good.

*   *   *   *   *

As we came home, we were looking forward to receiving our next brace of visitors. In Sue's last job she had had the privilege of working with some wonderful, amicable people in a closely knit team. Her closest ally had been Vicky, even though their two characters were like chalk and cheese. Vicky's idea of a fun evening would include various things that to Sue were off-limits; Vicky, in turn, was amazed to find that a devout Christian could be so down to earth, non-judgmental, and fun-loving like Sue. It was that sense of humour, coupled with the commitment of the team to doing a good job, that bound them together as buddies.

Their place of work had been a Woodland Burial Ground. Set in the heart of the New Forest, this peaceful haven was the setting for funerals for those who wished to be laid to rest in its tranquil surroundings. Each cortege of mourners in turn would approach the grounds at a carefully measured pace along the narrow, straight half-mile driveway, through open green countryside, until it passed through the gates of the wooded park and arrived at the burial centre. This beautiful round pavilion welcomed its solemn guests, its large windows illuminating the stage for burial services with a soft, pastoral light.

Sue's well-appointed, welcoming office was off to one side. From here she directed operations from behind her distinguished-looking desk and interviewed clients, who were ushered in hushed, respectful tones to sit in the comfortable cottage-style suite. On the wall hung paintings of woodland scenes, while the windows behind her overlooked a quiet corner of forest. All kinds of wildlife could often be seen quietly crossing the field of view: pheasants and partridges, pairs of green woodpeckers, and different species of deer.

To the rear of the building stood the chapel of rest, where the deceased waited in the wings for their final entrance to receive the farewells of their loved ones. The coffin was then carried out to the meadow for burial, an indigenous tree of their choice being planted in the place of a gravestone.

Next to the chapel lay the garden of remembrance, a simple plot with a single plaque to mark the resting place of those whose ashes had been buried there. The plant population, a dozen disconsolate rose bushes, shared its living space rather unsuccessfully with a far more flourishing colony of rabbits, which stubbornly resisted all Richard the groundsman's attempts at eviction.

One of the most amusing and, at the same time, taxing incidents in their work together occurred as the result of a double booking coinciding with the visit of a rather eccentric old lady. On the fateful day in question, the booking error was uncovered while Sue's attention was being given to the slightly odd, extremely fussy Ethel, who was reviewing the available plots in order to choose the final resting place of her recently deceased husband. The remainder of the afternoon then unfolded into something resembling a Brian Rix farce.

Sue was blissfully unaware of the double booking of the burial centre until Vicky and Glen appeared, running back and forth between it and the chapel of rest, carrying tables and refreshments. (Glen was Sue's most versatile colleague, whose duties varied from preparing the deceased for burial to welcoming the mourners to the memorial ceremonies, to digging and filling in the actual graves.) It had only been a few minutes earlier, when the officiating minister for the second service arrived unexpectedly, that Sue's unsuspecting friends had had to spring into action.

Usually the refreshments would have followed the service in the burial centre. Now Vicky and Glen had to suddenly switch venues while maintaining an air of calm and normality at all times in the customers' presence. As Sue was gently guiding her frail customer around the garden of remembrance, her thoughts were with her colleagues, and they exchanged smiles and grimaces.

Suddenly, several events coincided in a fraction of a second. The expression on Vicky's face turned to horror while Sue felt a sense of release in her right arm, with which she had been supporting her unsteady charge. Sue turned instinctively, only to see Ethel melting gracefully into an unconscious heap. Thankfully, Richard was only a few feet away, trying to revive the rabbit ridden roses. Before Ethel could reach the ground, Richard had smartly whipped a seat from beside the ailing bush and scooped her neatly into a comfortable sitting position. 'I'm going to be sick! I'm going to be sick!' Ethel muttered with all the strength she could muster. Vicky, who was now standing sympathetically alongside, ran for an appropriate receptacle.

By the time the troop of mourners were filing thoughtfully from the burial centre to their newly assigned and freshly prepared refreshment venue, Sue was poised discreetly, sick bowl at the ready. Should any of them have glanced to their left, they may have concluded from Sue's stooped posture and Ethel's forward inclination that the manager was directing the old lady's attention to some delicate wildflower hiding among the blades of grass at her feet.

No sooner had the transfer taken place than Glen suddenly emerged and said, 'Get out of the garden! There's a service about to start!'

A nod from Richard, and immediately they had lifted the chair and were carrying it with its unwilling occupant through the French window into the back of Sue's office, with Ethel shrieking all the while, 'I'm going to fall!' and clutching tightly on to her bowl.

As the presiding minister welcomed the new set of mourners, Sue was dialling for an ambulance, and the first party was tucking into a pleasant buffet. The latter was full of praise, complimenting their hosts on the efficient organisation and excellent facilities. 'This is such a lovely room to retire to—so light and airy, and what a beautiful view over the pond!'

The final snag that had to be overcome by Sue and her team was the reluctance of the ambulance driver to bring his vehicle down the approach road and round to the back of the building, where it was required. Glen was immediately dispatched to drive up to meet them. Thanks to his speedy intervention, by the time the emergency vehicle pulled up to relieve Sue and her staff of their troubled potential client, the second set of mourners had just vacated the burial centre, exiting left to the garden of remembrance. Thus they were able to bury the ashes of their departed loved one in the dignity and peace which normally reign over this corner of the New Forest. The ambulance crew greeted Ethel with a friendly familiarity that betrayed her infamous renown among the medical community. The vivid image of her still clutching tightly on to the sick bowl, while being lifted into the ambulance, has been imprinted indelibly on Sue's memory from that day 'til now.

Accordingly, it was with great anticipation that we awaited a visit from Vicky and her equally personable daughter, Katie. Ample amounts of food and wine were purchased with great thought for Vicky and Katie's tastes. The house was spring cleaned, the guest beds made, and the en-suite bathroom made pretty and perfumed, all in an effort to provide Sue's great friends with the warmest Lanzarote welcome possible.

Then disaster hit! Vicky and Katie were booked with Excel, who went bust precisely seven days before their take-off was due. The only flights then available would have cost Vicky the pretty sum of £1,200! It was a bitter disappointment for us all. The stockpiles of victuals and beautifully done-up visitors' quarters only served to remind us virtually hourly of the absence of two very special people whose presence we had both been anticipating with such excitement. That was a great blow for Sue and underlined and highlighted in bold capital letters the fact of her missing not just Vicky and Katie but all her friends she had been separated from so suddenly and decisively.

Thankfully, we had some great new friends down the road to console us. Shortly after moving into our pristine new home in Playa Blanca, we learned through mutual friends of a lady who, like us, had recently moved over from England and, looking for like-minded Christians, was keen to make contact with us. After a few frustrated attempts to link up, we finally found her home, a few minutes' walk down the hill and around the corner, on a new estate, like our own, aptly named *Villas Blancas*.

Marika turned out to have come from Liverpool, had installed herself with her eleven-year-old daughter, Catalina, and was waiting for her husband, Denis, to join her in a couple of months. We soon found Marika to be a fascinating person, with whom we had much in common. Marika's name is actually Greek but her exotic looks betray more of her mother's African race than that of her Greek father. As we sat in her beautifully appointed lounge, with its views across the invitingly blue water of her swimming pool towards the red mountains, we quickly discovered that she also spoke French, her mother having been remarried to a French man, so that Marika had spent her childhood in Kinshasa, Zaire, and Brazzaville in the Congo.

This interesting mixture of cultures has left its mark linguistically. According to Marika, and this is backed up firmly by her family, in her most vexed moments she resorts to her first language, Lingala, a dialect from the Congo. In our company this has never happened to my knowledge. When we're together, usually on a Friday evening on an average once a fortnight, enjoying one another's company and lively conversation over a meal, Marika will often break into her second language, which pleases me, not having many opportunities for French conversation in this part of the world. On these occasions the topic is usually the food that we're lingering over.

Denis took early retirement from his high-powered job in information technology at the Liverpool Docks. He and Marika have thrown themselves into the island's cosmopolitan culture through their involvement in a variety of local churches. Marika has quickly mastered the language. She may not care too much for the grammar, but she's absolutely fluent. I guess it helps that she already speaks three other languages with the same degree of fluency. I think of them as bridge people, which is very appropriate given the name of their church back in Liverpool, Bridge Chapel. As we catch up with one another over dinner, they keep us informed of the latest developments in at least three different local churches, only one of which is English speaking. It's also nice that they're not in our church, because we can have a relaxed friendship that's not so easy between the pastor and members of his flock.

It goes without saying that indispensable elements in the experience of French hospitality are the aperitif, the wine accompanying each course, and the digestif at the end. To put it bluntly, alcohol! In Normandy, where we have had the pleasure of partaking in numerous such feasts, there is even a custom they call *le trou Normand* (the Norman hole). This involves the locally produced, and highly potent apple brandy, or Calvados. A quick shot before each course creates a *trou normand*—room for the dish that follows. We all have our limit, and for me that's not particularly high. But, as the Bible says, 'Wine gladdens the heart' and is an appreciated part of our gastronomic get-togethers.

However, I have to say here that my favourite drink is a simple glass of cool, refreshing water. In all my years of exercising in various gyms it's been impressed upon me the importance of maintaining a good level of hydration. It's supposed to be particularly good for the nervous system. So, whenever we arrive at Denis and Marika's and have seated ourselves at their patio table with some tasty nibbles, my preferred aperitif is pure and simple water. Over the months, however, I've come to realise something. As I start to relax into the evening, sip my drink, and chomp on the odd olive or potato crisp, looking around at what everyone else is imbibing, my attention is invariably drawn to the wine bottle. I just have a fascination for the labels. For me, the poetic descriptions in Spanish and sometimes also in French and German and even English, evoke enticing images and flavours, thus arousing an intense curiosity. It's at this point that Denis usually offers me a sip from his glass. I don't like to pass on any germs I might have so a quick waft of the wine's bouquet under my finely tuned nose is enough to persuade me that a glass of *vino* would be a great addition to my H_2O.

Sue presented us with an appetising and delicious supper, and our friends helped us eat up some of the surplus rations that had been bought in for Vicky's visit. Both Denis and I are blessed with wives who also happen to be great cooks. In addition, through our contact with French culture, we had both learned how to buck the British trend towards throwing the food down one's neck at high speed, and take time to savour the flavours, textures, and sensations, while engaging in the sort of cheerful banter that characterised our times with our new chums.

One of the things we particularly appreciate about Denis is his remarkable ability to involve absolutely anybody in animated conversation. So whenever we have particularly troublesome visitors, an evening in the company of Denis and Marika is guaranteed to provide some essential light relief. Normally though, I prefer to keep Denis to myself. As he shares with me our common interest in politics and world events, computers, and other typically male topics, it's refreshing to engage with his combination of intelligence and down-to-earth Liverpudlian common sense.

As we tucked in, Denis was saying that the older he gets, the more patriotic he gets. He had been watching the Trooping of the

Colour, a piece of English pageantry that dates back to the seventeenth century, which has become an annual spectacle marking the sovereign's accession to the throne.

'Well, it reminds me, I suppose, of a proud part of our history. It's about pride isn't it? And I think, when somebody looks back in five hundred years' time, they'll say "What's Britain achieved?" and I think they'll say, "Not very much". But if you look back two, three, four hundred years, we've got a lot to be proud of … I could write for the *Daily Telegraph*, you know!' He chuckled.

There was great merriment as I recorded our conversation for possible inclusion in this volume. Marika seemed to be suggesting how nice it would be for me to play back my recording at a later date, just to hear her voice!

'No, I meant it would be good for Denis if I went away, I could leave him instructions—to put the machine on twice a week, to make sure to eat—but proper food, not just a bit of cheese and a glass of wine and a piece of bread'.

'That sounds better', Denis chimed in, 'and it's got to be red wine and hard cheese, Sue. *C'est parfait, monsieur!'*

'Oh, so you're expecting my wife to feed you', I exclaimed.

'Yes, because she bought soft cheese, and you know brie's very bad for my heart', he joked.

'Yes, but are you assuming that my wife is going to look after you if your wife goes away?' I probed further.

'Oh, hopefully, yeah. Hopefully I'll get invited for my dinner every evening, and Sue will make chocolate puddings every night'.

We all had a good chuckle about that!

'Honestly!' Sue concluded the banter.

*　　*　　*　　*　　*

As the summer arrived, although we were settled in our home and work, our household still lacked something. When we first moved out here, one of the issues we had to face was, 'What do we do with the cat?' Having seen a number of cats lying lifelessly by the side of the notoriously dangerous Lanzarote roads, I felt it would be a great shame if, having gone to the expense and trouble of transporting the poor creature, it fell prey to such a sad fate. Sue was rather more reluctant to leave our fluffy feline companion, Frilly, back in England. However, she finally agreed philosophically, and our newly married daughter, Ali, helpfully gave the abandoned moggy a new home.

Sue still felt the sacrifice though. We joked to our friends that, since it was in order to serve the Lord that we left England and, therefore, the cat, that he would reward us one hundred times—with one hundred cats in the place we were going to. Hence, we advised our friends in a parting letter that the way to find our new abode when visiting the island would be to ask the question, '¿Dónde está la casa con los cien gatos?' ('Where is the house with a hundred cats?')

In future letters I kept people back home up to date with our progress toward the one hundred target. Early editions displayed photos of various candidates for the job of replacing Frilly, now comfortably ensconced in Ali and Tim's new home. Still, no suitable replacement could be found, and it wasn't until fully a year after installation in our own new home that we heard of a strikingly similar specimen, which had been left by her owner in a cattery eleven months previously and never reclaimed.

And so it was that Millie came to take up residence with us. Like Frilly, she was a long-haired tortoiseshell, only rather a darker smoky chocolate colour than Frilly's lighter grey. Both cats were also very talkative, always greeting either one of us with a welcoming meow, and responding vocally when spoken to.

Maybe it was to do with Millie's long stay in the cattery—nearly a year would be approaching a third of her little life—without much in the way of human companionship, but whatever it was, she was in no way what one would call a lap cat. The closest she would get to my lap was when she wanted to change position from one arm of the sofa to the other, and I was sitting en route. It was on these occasions that I had to be careful that a paw thrusting her entire mass (a whisker light of a whopping sixteen pounds) from the lowest point of her path to her resting place on the arm next to me didn't find itself planted in my unprotected private parts.

Millie's weight problem was also a bit of a worry. Whatever we tried, her tubby form continued to tip the scales at alarmingly high readings. The first weight-loss programme we attempted comprised exercise and controlled intake of food. By making sure she went out at night to 'play with the mouses', and measuring in a cup her biscuits for the day, we thought her furry figure would soon become more streamlined. But Millie wasn't having this. When the day's supply of biscuits was exhausted, she would start up the most annoyingly loud and relentless squalling, as if she was about to die of starvation!

When it comes to cats, we have a fair few years of experience, and when it comes to this cat in particular, one doesn't need to be a genius to outsmart her. Thus, Sue's cunning ploy was to place a bowl of biscuits in front of the unsuspecting creature, but not the usual variety. Instead, these were the cheapest supermarket's own brand available. 'If she's really that desperate she'll eat these!' Her bluff called, the greedy creature would sniff a bit at the unappetising offering before, much to our relief, quietly turning away.

A bit later, though, she'd be back with a repeat performance. She may have lacked in brains, but she more than made up for it with her dramatic talent, that's for sure! Of course, her bowl was already full at this time so, accordingly, the procedure we adopted was to lift the bowl from the floor and remove its contents for a split second before pouring it back in such a manner as to produce the familiar rattle of biscuit against bowl that would trigger the desired response in the wailing beast, viz. 'Shut up and eat'.

Of course, every cat has its own personality; Millie's redeeming feature is that she will allow you to stroke her and groom her with very little fuss or objection, unlike some cats we've known. We've even wondered at times if she had a bit of the rag doll breed in her. Other cats we've owned, or to be more accurate, that have owned us, have had varying natures, all with different pluses and minuses. Tigger was the first. We got her from some good friends who lived near Newbury. She'd been rejected by her mother and was a tiny scrap of a thing when we first brought her home. Her grey fluffy coat and piercing blue eyes made her the sort of kitten you see in pictures on boxes of chocolates and birthday cards.

Sue and I had just got married and moved into a rented bungalow five minutes' walk from her mum and dad. On our regular Saturday evening visits, Tigger would ride happily like a little Joey in the front pocket of Sue's kagool. (For those not old enough to remember, a kagool was a shower-proof nylon top everybody used to wear in the seventies.) Sue's mum, I remember, was particularly fond of little Tigger, and quite disappointed, even dismayed, when she outgrew her pouch and had to stay at home.

Yes, Tigger was definitely the family favourite. Having had her from so small, Sue always felt she was 'her cat'. Both our children's first words were 'Didder' as they stretched a little hand out towards the unsuspecting family pet in order to grab another handful of her long, soft fur. Even my feelings for her bubbled up when I went to collect her from the vet for the very last time. The poor creature had become ill after eating a mouse, one of the bones having punctured her insides. So it was that at ten years old, her life was suddenly ended. I can still remember the tears rising and the flush of embarrassment as I choked on the words, 'I've come to collect my cat'.

There followed in quick succession a few attempted replacements for the recently perished puss. Midge, who sported a fine white coat and a smart stripy tail, betrayed his appearance by behaving in the most mischievous ways. My overriding memory of him is glimpsing his furry haunches and tail slipping from sight into the kitchen swing bin as he helped himself to a customary unauthorised snack. You can imagine our relief when he disappeared without a trace soon after his arrival!

Holly and Lacey followed Midge. They were six months old by the time they joined our family and, having been born on a farm, didn't take to life in a relatively busy suburban street. I found myself presented with the first lifeless form and then the other, by different neighbours, as they came to grief under the wheels of passing vehicles.

The next candidate for Herman family cat was a black kitten, the sole survivor of a litter with chocolate and tabby markings. By this time we'd run out of imagination for names, and all we could think of was 'P' for pussycat. On her first trip to the vet the comment was 'Why P? Is that what she does?' P had a very sweet nature; she was disarmingly affectionate and let our two small children do almost anything to her without complaining. If they went too far, a gentle warning smack of the paw was enough to bring any shenanigans to a mutually agreeable halt. She related to Sue with equal affection, to the point that whenever the latter felt the need for a good cry, P would appear without fail, bringing her own brand of comfort.

So you can imagine my horror one day, when it seemed that at last a new feline friend had come to stay, as I opened the front door to hear the neighbours through the tall separating hedge say, 'It's next door's cat, just cover it up!' I quickly realised they were burying what P didn't require anymore, rather than what she definitely did require in the shape of her furry black body.

We haven't reached the one hundred cat mark yet. In fact we stopped at one for reasons that will shortly be revealed.

*   *   *   *   *

The summer passed and soon it was October. As Paula clocked up seven months in hospital, we went off to Madrid to see her again and enjoy another stay. We decided to surprise her. It was fun calling her from the baggage collection area at Madrid airport to tell her that we were on our way to visit her at the hospital.

We found her looking better than she had in March, and determined to be back home for Christmas. I marvelled at her good humour as she regaled us with incredible stories of the contrasting levels of care she had received from different members of the nursing staff.

What's so appealing about Spain's capital city is the convenient arrangement of alluring shops next to the olde-worlde streets full of interesting restaurants offering delicious menus, all a stone's throw from the beautiful Retiro Park. Known as the 'lungs of Madrid', it is flanked by a cluster of the world's greatest art galleries.

The centre of the city, and indeed of the whole country, is a huge bustling square, the Puerta del Sol. From here you can take a pleasant stroll up through a pedestrian only street to the Plaza Mayor, a veritable tourist haven where the hubbub of animated conversation and live music complements the tranquil backdrop of the eighteenth-century architecture. The focal point of the spacious cobbled square is a statue of an imposing Spanish king rearing up on his royal mount ready to engage some imaginary enemy.

The main feature around two corners of the quadrangle is the café bars where people like us sit and drink in the atmosphere as well as an incidental glass of something liquid. For us, it's the sort of place where we love to linger, and as time slips by unnoticed, and the hunger pangs begin, we don't mind succumbing to the temptation of an ample variety of more solid sustenance.

On this occasion, it is Paula's presence that has drawn us to Madrid. And so far, fingers crossed, we've always been blessed with fabulous weather—warm autumn sunshine or long sunny summer days followed by warm bright evenings under the lamplight of our favourite square.

This time we're treating ourselves to two nights in a hotel we discovered on our last trip. I remark to Sue, 'This city doesn't seem as foreign as it used to'. It's not such a different experience as it was the first couple of times. But that isn't such a bad thing. The cheerful 'welcome back' of the hotel receptionist reinforces the comfortable feeling of being at home.

We slip immediately into a late routine, essential to enjoying the evening entertainment, since the evening meal is served from around nine, and the compulsory visit to a flamenco *tablao* is usually impossible before eleven. Thankfully, our hotel of choice lends itself admirably to sleeping in. Situated on a quiet corner next to the Plaza Mayor, the room opens onto a central shaft that allows in very little daylight. Hence, it is customarily nine a.m. before we even know the day has started. For us, relaxation, savouring the experience, and enjoying each other's company is the name of the game. Accordingly, there follows a leisurely buffet breakfast, which, by the time we finish, could arguably qualify as an abundant brunch.

Strictly speaking, the morning is now nearly gone. However, lunch in Madrid doesn't occur before two p.m. Our 'morning' then consists of a visit to our favourite Spanish department store, aptly named *Corte Inglés*, which translates as English style. While Sue browses a variety of sections from the delicatessen in the basement to the well-stocked racks of ladies' fashions of the upper storeys, I can be reliably located in the expansive *espacio de música*, a whole music shop within a shop. I could, and indeed sometimes do, gladly listen to Spanish and Latin music all day.

The shopping over with, it's time to quickly drop our purchases in our room, before strolling down the hill along a new route of wide avenues, cobbled streets, and inviting plazas, until we reach our afternoon haunt—the Retiro Gardens. Here we alternate between the lightly shaded tables of the outdoor cafés and the wooden benches lining the broad walkway along one side of the boating lake reminiscent of the one found in Hyde Park.

Call us boring, but we find it just the perfect spot to sit and lose ourselves in a book, scribble some recollections in a notebook bought specially for the occasion, watch the world go by, or just '*plane*', as the French would say—a succinct little word that describes the pleasant drifting sensation associated with doing absolutely nothing. After a few hours of doing nothing, stomachs start their teatime rumble and our minds turn adeptly to the subject of food, and in particular to the meal we've come to call 'first tea' in honour of the hobbits from one of our favourite family films, *Lordy Rings,* as we termed it affectionately.

Even more in particular, when in Madrid, our minds are never far from the most delicious of all patisseries and tea rooms known to Herman-kind. Bearing the name of La Mallorquina, this palace of creamy pleasures stands splendidly on a prominent corner of the Puerta del Sol, situated very conveniently and even calculatedly three minutes down the hill from our hotel. The queen of all cream cakes is literally that—*la reina de nata*. In the form of a pyramid, it is basically cream with a hint of chocolaty sponge, dusted lightly with icing sugar, a firm favourite of Sue's.

After a disappointing meal in a cheap Galician restaurant, and in a renewed effort to create that special holiday meal experience, the next evening we inquired carefully with the receptionist where we might find a good, juicy piece of proper steak. Having then investigated further on the Internet, the choice was made: La Cabaña, an Argentinian restaurant we were assured from all sources would not disappoint. The only drawback: it wasn't open until nine p.m. By eight we were ready to eat, and to complicate things further, it had unexpectedly started to rain. Our receptionist informed us cheerily that this was the start of a spectacular storm, and that, if it was anything like the one they had had two weeks earlier, there would be both sheet and forked lightning, striking the taller buildings in an entertaining display.

We launched ourselves into the rainy streets hoping to find an earlier opening eatery than the one we'd already selected. Forty minutes later, our impromptu tour of the local area brought us to a clear conclusion: Madrid evenings before nine p.m. are all about one thing—tapas! Everywhere we looked offered tapas dishes, including *pinchos, porciones de pulpo,* and *raciones de rabo.* Not a steak in sight! As Sue's desperation grew, I gritted my teeth in ever-greater determination. Finally, having wrenched her away from the windows of several inappropriate restaurants, I dragged her into the nearest place that could serve us a drink while we waited for the clock to tick slowly round to 8.55. It didn't matter that it was a shabby Spanish imitation of KFC.

We arrived at La Cabaña with great anticipation on the dot of nine o'clock. I do so appreciate service with a smile. One waitress in particular smiled pleasantly every time she spoke to us, while another was so miserable looking that I joked to Sue that she was proof of what our parents used to warn us when we were small and pulled such a face, that if the wind should change direction, our faces would be permanently deformed into a disfiguring scowl! Toward the end of the meal, I realised there were actually two waitresses who looked so alike that they must have been twins or, at least, sisters. The only difference appeared to be that, while one was wearing glasses with black frames, the other's frames were white.

It reminded me of an amusing occasion some years ago, when we used to enjoy frequenting a wonderfully authentic French restaurant in Brockenhurst, just beside the school where we first met. The young waiter who attended us that evening was very personable and chatty, telling us all about life back in the French Alps. Nonetheless he seemed a little forgetful, as if he were suffering from some sort of short-term memory loss. As the meal progressed, our puzzlement grew at how he was unable to recall details of the short conversation we'd just had between one appearance at the table and the next. Finally, at the end of the proceedings he presented himself for the final time ... along with his twin brother! The funniest thing of all was that one twin had a beard, while the other was clean-shaven. We had both failed to notice our *garçon*'s sudden gains and losses of facial hair that had appeared to accompany the very particular dementia. Probably a good thing, or it might have spooked us to the point of putting us off even the feast of delightful French cuisine we had just enjoyed.

CHAPTER 8

We Get By with a Little Help from Our Friends

As November arrived, it was the turn of my older sister, Wendy, to come and stay with her husband. To Richard's discomfort, they managed to coincide with a four-day period of *calima*, where the thermometer touches thirty-four° Celsius (ninety-two° Fahrenheit). My abiding memory is of Richard sitting in our front room, saying, 'I don't do hot!'

On the other hand, what he did do most excellently was seek out and appreciate the local produce, introducing us to all manner of cheeses, wines, seafood, and other less easily identified delicacies. The highlight of their stay came when Richard took Sue's place in the kitchen and conjured up a tasty paella.

Wendy is simply a pleasure to have around, with her easy laugh and calm, quiet disposition. She complements Richard in his flamboyant cooking exploits, always on hand to clear up after him in the kitchen without a word of complaint.

*   *   *   *   *

As Christmas approached, Sue was getting pretty down about her job. The drawbacks to her working environment at Jardines Playa had been steadily piling on the stress. She was in tears most days, and I was worried that she was heading for a nervous breakdown. The 'make do and mend' attitude of the management might seem trivial to the outsider. The door would normally be propped open with a box full of brochures. Of course, with exposure to the hot Lanzarote sunshine, over time the cardboard rotted and the 'make do' doorstop collapsed, spilling brochures over the threshold and into the street. Never mind, the system was promptly and ingeniously 'mended' by the application of a piece of wire somebody found by ferreting through a cupboard full of assorted bits and pieces kept 'just in case', at the back of the office.

Matters were made worse by the fact that the boss would bend over backward to please his customers while inclining himself forward over his staff and breathing fire down their necks. The contrast could not have been greater. However good the service they gave to the clients, and however delighted that person might have been, the boss would invariably find fault with the way the arrangements had been made and storm around the office in such a rage that Sue's colleagues gave him the nickname 'Purple Head'.

All this meant that to survive in the surroundings for an extended period of time, Sue's coworkers had to have skins as thick as a proverbial rhino. Many was the occasion when Purple Head would stand in the middle of the office and harangue his unfortunate employees over subjects such as the necessity of quoting insurance premiums, even when the customer had stated clearly that they had already made their own provision. It was only six months after Sue had finished working there, when she was comparing notes with an ex-colleague, that they both realised that one effect of this disturbing experience had been that, whenever the telephone rang, they would pray fervently under their breath, 'Please don't book!'

As time went on, the accumulated distress caused by working in such a hostile environment took its toll on Sue. Her confidence reached an all-time low, and I was finding it difficult to bring her comfort in the midst of her frequent tearful outbursts. It was no good looking for comfort in stroking the cat either. Unlike P, who would come running when she heard Sue crying, Millie the cat was totally unsympathetic, and her unsociable nature just seemed to emphasise the desperation Sue was feeling.

Not only did the cat fail to do her job, she even added to the stress. She was showing signs of an infection, and medical attention was necessary. We have always found bundling a cat into a box to take it to the vet a stressful experience. With Millie, this was doubly so. First, Millie actually took up as much room as two normal-sized cats. Secondly, our struggle with the cat seemed like the last straw on top of Sue's trouble at work. Having squeezed her into the cat box, we finally managed to get her to a very pleasant young lady vet, who had just started practising in the town. The latter was very impressed with our ability to get such a fat cat into such a small box! As she tried to weigh the awkward creature, Millie fought against her, and the reading from the scales oscillated wildly up and down. Finally she was pronounced as a full 6.3 kilos (14 pounds). 'She could do with losing a good kilo!' the vet commented. 'There's so much fat there, I can't feel her organs'.

Thankfully, the administration of antibiotic by syringe cured the infection. Nevertheless, the weight problem remained. There was only one thing for it. I took over the task of feeding our fat feline and forbade Sue to give her anything by mouth. A week later I weighed Millie myself, using a more accurate method. By simply holding the animal in my arms and subtracting my weight from that of the two of us together, I arrived at an astonishing 6.9 kilos. The vet had underestimated the obese beast's weight by some way! The drastic reduction to her food intake entailed a proportionate increase in her pestering and wailing for food, as well as her wrapping herself around our legs every time we went near the kitchen. We really didn't need any more cats like that!

All the same, there was some light relief provided by our weekly visits to Denis and Marika's house to follow the latest edition of the British *X Factor*. To be honest, I get a bit out of touch with what's happening in my native England. So it's good to be kept up to date by people who have English TV, as well as being good fun and a break from the Spanish monopoly of our own TV set.

Marika in particular gets completely involved in the latest edition of the *X Factor*, and we all enjoy a lively and light-hearted exchange of opinions about the presenters, the contestants, and the show in general.

In the auditions stage, Rachel from Wales epitomised the kind of contestant we love to hate. We grimaced along with Danni Minogue as Rachel sang, and greeted Rachel's assessment of her own performance with total incredulity.

'That was good, wasn't it; let's face it!' she pronounced.

'No! You've got a really bad attitude, sweetheart'. Simon Cowell corrected her flatly. And we agreed!

Louis Walsh's return as a judge, having been absent at the start, gave the show that essential ingredient we call *shoutability*. I particularly enjoy responding to his comments with my own, such as, 'What a load of baloney!'

Although the new presenter, Dermot O'Leary, didn't impress us to start with, we soon learned to appreciate his irreverent handling of the judges as he brought them down a notch. 'Go Dermot!' we shouted encouragingly.

In all, the show provided a wonderful escape. As the final approached, we were especially intrigued by the survival of an enigmatic character by the name of Rhydian Roberts with his curious sticky-up white hair and operatic voice.

Meanwhile, Paula's stay in hospital in Madrid, initially predicted as six weeks, had turned into nine months, so that just before we left to spend Christmas with our family in the United Kingdom, Paula had returned to convalesce in Arrecife hospital. To our surprise and delight, she appeared one morning at church. Now reduced to seven stone and leaning heavily on a stick for support, her frail frame was that of an infirm old lady. Nevertheless, despite her obvious physical weakness, it was a thrill to have her back with us and on the road, however bumpy and long that might be, to a full recovery.

*　　*　　*　　*　　*

As we began 2008, we were looking forward to another visit from Guy and Hazel. One can easily get the impression, having taken the 'north' coach tour one day and the 'south' the next, that's all there is—'I've done the island'. Indeed, Guy and Hazel had 'done it'. Nevertheless they keep coming back. We were in the middle of the longest, coldest, wettest winter in living memory, when they arrived aboard a 'small' cruise ship docking in the Puerto de los Marmoles for the day. In fact, they'd started their exploration of our corner of the Atlantic with a flight to Madeira, about five hundred miles to the north of us. It being their first such excursion, Hazel had chosen a smaller vessel, which engendered in me some frightening visions of our unfortunate friends being tossed around in a bucket of a boat and turning a frightful pale green. Furthermore, the day they arrived the forecast was for heavy rain, following the heavy swell that had prevailed at sea during the preceding week or so.

So it was with great relief that we received a smiling Hazel and Guy on the quayside the third Thursday morning in January. Guy was full of praise for the ample facilities of the ship, comparing it rather favourably with the 'Grey Funnel Line'—the military means of marine transport during his thirty-year career in the army. With the wet weather forecast, and taking into account their feeling that they had 'done' our little island many years ago, we decided to try to show them something different.

Before the rains were due to arrive at around lunchtime, I worked out that a little tour of the commercial heart of Arrecife would give them the opportunity to see the 'less touristy' side of Lanzarote life and a pleasant stroll around the extensive pedestrian zone of the capital, with its variety of shops and cafés and openings onto the charming El Charco, as they call the old harbour here. El Charco is a charming place in itself. The original architecture stands with its simple colour scheme of blue fittings on white facades, framing and embracing two sides of the quiet harbour, with its smattering of small boats and sprinkling of wildlife in the form of sandpipers and other birds that know how to thrive on the sandy part of its shoreline. This is the heart of the old town of Arrecife, closely connected to the pretty old church of San Gines by a higgledy-piggledy patchwork of narrow side streets.

While Sue guided our friends' discovery of the commercial face of Arrecife, I was able to catch up with a few chores related to my working life, which has to continue even though it is tempting to down tools and take time off every time another friend or family member shows their face. Having finished off my working morning with a visit to the solicitor's office, we moved on, driving back toward the new port along the seafront road that joins the old with the new, winding its way past the ancient fort known as the Castillo de San José. This monument became a lunchtime stop. Its chambers, which originally housed coastal defences against marauding pirates, have been beautifully converted into an art gallery at the level of the entrance from the small car park. An impressive spiral staircase takes the visitor down through a stairwell whose walls are used as an effective background to show off a variety of large-scale art.

Time was limited, so we entered straight from the outside, skirting around the ground-level gallery and descending the rocky lava cliff through a garden that merited closer inspection. This would have revealed the path laid in a perfect pattern of swirling smooth black pebbles of identical shape and size along with a simple and effective arrangement of plants, edged with red lava boulders. As we continued down, aloe vera with bright vermilion flowers stood like stranded upturned octopuses in the company of closely clipped red hibiscus and other bushes valiantly tolerating the strong salty winds. Rounding the corner, we were led onto a narrow cliff-side gallery appropriately fenced with sea chains that had been put to more strenuous work in their maritime past. The rugged approach with its exposure to the refreshing sea breeze had allowed some brief moments of bracing exercise before we entered the welcome refuge offered by the eating quarters of the ingeniously restored monument.

The restaurant comprises a large cavernous area, lit on one side by a long curving wall of clear glass windows that allows an unrestricted view beyond the harbour to the right and over towards the modern port to the left. These panoramas are typical of the Manrique monuments where he's built on existing structures, both man-made and natural, bringing out the potential of the island's *patrimonio*, its extraordinary cultural and geographical heritage. In this case he chose an idyllic spot for this quiet and spacious restaurant.

Turning to the inside, the décor is just as striking. One friend described it as like walking into a Walter Matthau movie, with its seventies feel and jazzy Muzak. The very smart black-and-tan colour scheme enhances the distinguished air of the establishment. Black cloths cover the serried ranks of tables capable of seating a small planeload of travellers. Not being on the coach tour routes, however, means we've always been able to enjoy its facilities in near exclusion.

The smart straight lines of the black rectangular volcanic stone pillars contrast with the informality of those in the upper café bar of Jameos del Agua, another of Manrique's creations in the north of the island, and have no doubt been the silent witnesses to many dinners pawed over disdainfully by the rich and famous. In the same way, joists hewn perfectly from the same sort of rock run at precise right angles to their upright counterparts.

Alongside the black, the tan element runs through the wooden floorboards and lampshades. The latter are extraordinarily intricate, and I'm not doing justice to the handiwork that's gone into each one when I confess that they remind me of upside-down baskets. The low bar that runs almost the whole length of one side is a lustrous, richly coloured piece of wood they call Riga and we call Scots Pine. Its elongated L-shape is exactly matched by the array of twenty-four lampshades clinging to the ceiling.

By the time we had studied the menu, with its inviting variety of local fare and entertaining translations into English, we were ready to tuck into a meal of grilled vegetables, fish, and onion omelette, and an abundance of freshly prepared potato chips. A satisfying yet simple feast finished, in my case, with my favourite sweet—ice cream, of course: vanilla, chocolate, and *gofio*, the local toasted cereal acclaimed with all manner of health-giving properties and whose flavour reminds me of my childhood favourite sugar puffs.

We now had a couple of hours to complete our unveiling of the hitherto unknown delights of the island with a quick trip around the Arrecife ring road to the stylish Deiland shopping centre on the far side of the town. The centre is constructed around two large open atriums, forming an L-shape, and includes a wide plaza, the stage for regular cultural events in the evenings. For us, it's an opportune place to shop for clothes and shoes, stop for a coffee, and catch up with Gemma, who's been serving at the open central café for as long as we've been here, as well as take in the occasional film.

Our first visit to the Spanish cinema was fairly typical of the pattern we set for ourselves. We arrived expectantly at the ticket counter with no queue, paid our five euros each before passing by the snack counter to purchase the obligatory nibbles and drinks that complete any worthwhile cinema-going experience. Inquiring as to the variety of popcorn on sale, we discovered that, as is not unusual for the simple scheme of life out here, there were two choices: salty or nothing. After that, we would preface our film viewings with a quick spin by the snack shelves of the Hiperdino supermarket placed carefully, at the greatest distance possible, in the opposite corner of the centre. Thankfully, they don't mind us taking in our own food; 'sandwiches in the cinema' is not a source of embarrassment in the relaxed culture of the Canaries.

For our visitors, Deiland offers an opportunity to catch up with a bit of holiday shopping. We split up into guys and gals. Having swapped the customary jokes about the danger of letting our wives loose with the credit card, Guy and I headed first for some clothing bargains in the *rebajas*, the sales. It was difficult to judge sizes, as we tried on different shirts over the top of the clothes we were already wearing. Nevertheless, at three euros for a decent shirt, one could afford the odd inaccuracy.

The result for me was one rather baggy black shirt together with a very smartly tailored sky-blue one which sported a distinguished white vertical stripe. I should have got two! Guy, on the other hand, was obviously feeling a bit less adventurous. The shirt that looked rather tight over his own apparel probably would have fitted perfectly. With hindsight we really should have used the *probadores*, the fitting rooms!

The next shop was more successful from my friend's point of view, as he carefully chose a new bag for his Olympus digital SLR, along with a memory card to accommodate another thousand pictures of the many worthy sights offered by the outstanding and varied beauty of our corner of the ocean.

CHAPTER 9

Sandwiches in the Sun

As spring finally arrived, Mark and Julie were preparing to hand over the reins of the church. Having laboured sacrificially for eight years to lay the foundation of a solid community, they were ready to return to England.

'I don't want you to suffer the way we have', Mark commented. As the church members met under his pastorship for the last time, he recommended that I should be paid a half-time salary. 'That should take care of the basics, and your translation work can then pay for the odd holiday and meal out'.

At the same time, the wedding company I had been working with was expanding, and Sue was even given a trial run, organising the coach to pick up wedding guests from various corners of the island, deposit them safely in Teguise, and bring them back to the reception at Puerto Calero. It was like a dream come true, as we both attended the reception at the distinguished Amura restaurant, sitting on its wide terrace on a beautiful, sunny spring evening, overlooking the marina, chatting with the friendly guests, and enjoying the live music provided by the best flamenco artists on the island. Thus, with my promotion to pastor and the promise of bits and pieces of casual work from different friends with a variety of businesses, Sue was finally able to seize the opportunity to escape from her infernal employer.

A couple of months earlier, the café on the corner opposite the church premises had become available for new management. It was a thriving business, and this seemed an ideal opportunity for us to reach out into the community. For one thing, we would be able to provide a safe place for the numerous youngsters to congregate—much better than the local nightclubs where young teens normally hung out. In addition, our resident chef, Paul, would be able to exercise his talents in the cause. The recently baptised Cathy would run the front of house, and Sue would even be able to earn a few euros casually, helping out during the busier periods.

As we bade farewell to Mark, Julie, and Naomi, the mantle of pastor fell fairly and squarely upon my shoulders. I soon started to feel its weight. As we were watching one of our favourite TV series on DVD, a quote from one of the characters summed up my feelings. The programme was *24*. Toward the end of season six, the character of US vice president finds himself having to step up as acting president in the middle of a national crisis. Up to that point he has been very critical of the president's decisions. Now he has the responsibility himself, he observes wryly, 'It all looks so clear until you're the one having to take responsibility'.

Sue and I decided our priority was to get the church looking outward and focused on drawing in new people. To this end, we planned a series of social events to which people could invite their friends, family, and neighbours to join in the fun and discover the pleasure of spending time with church members. Then they would realise that we didn't all have two heads, and didn't eat our own children! And maybe they would be less shy about joining us for worship on a Sunday morning.

Thus the café became the focus of the church community. A successful quiz night was followed by Paul putting on his own highly entertaining version of *Ready Steady Cook*. His audience was astounded as he produced one extraordinary dish after another from the random ingredients presented to him. Having invented an array of starters and main courses, including a wonderful spicy pork fricassee, he moved on to the desserts. A herby cream and white-chocolate mousse rounded off the evening's exploits.

The arrival of Ian White, an aspiring young journalist looking to establish himself on the island, brought further blessing. His articles about different folk and their adventures were published in the Canarian press, and the account of Paul's dramatic conversion even reached the *Baptist Times* in the United Kingdom. Ian opened the story, 'A top chef has told how he turned his life around after going from working with TV's Marco Pierre White to sleeping on a Lanzarote beach'. A few people even came looking for Paul to hear the story from the man himself, while Cathy took every opportunity to tell of her newfound faith.

May was an eventful month. Joe, a friend of Cathy's and successful timeshare salesman, unfortunately came to the end of a long illness, and I was called upon to conduct the funeral. Whenever we direct such a ceremony, we always look upon it as the celebration of a life. Joe had been well liked, so it was my privilege to paint an affectionate portrait of a loveable, larger-than-life character. His daughter, ex-wife, and brother-in-law, who formed the mourning family, were all appreciative of our efforts in their own particular way.

'You don't know what effect you have on people!' Misha said as we sat out on the terrace by the church café following the bun fight.

She was right; I didn't. I knew what she meant though; this was an affirmation of my pastoral manner and made quite an impact, coming as it did just a month into my new role.

It was good to know we had given Joe a good send-off and brought real comfort to those who had lost a loved one, whose life had been cut tragically short. I reflected again on my mixed feelings about these occasions. I hate seen people's distress in the depths of bereavement, yet it is a wonderful thing to be in a position to bring comfort at such a time.

* * * * *

The second big event was rather more upbeat. When Phil from the squash club announced he was shortly to be sixty-five, I was amazed. He has so much energy that it was hard to grasp he had reached retirement age. Amazing! In fact, 'amazing' is his favourite word, found frequently on his lips as he gives his usual spirited and highly engaging account of the latest anecdote.

Phil's son, Andy, and Portuguese daughter in law, Paula, had organised a surprise party for the landmark birthday occasion. It was to start at three p.m. Unfortunately, having noticed the tyres looking a bit squishy on Sue's car, I had held us up by attempting to remedy the situation at the local *gasolinera*. The final straw came when, upon noticing that one of the valve caps had gone AWOL, I enquired of the man behind the desk in the shop as to whether valve caps were sold there. He carried on writing for a few seconds. Admittedly, the desk was some six feet or so behind the empty sales counter, but the several seconds he took to respond to my cheery 'Hola!' could not be accounted for entirely by the slower pace of absolutely everything in rural Spain, right down to the speed of sound!

His glaring and rather aggressive glance in my direction, accompanied with a snapped 'No!' quickly conveyed the clear message he wished to send: 'What do you think you're doing in my shop, you stupid person? Can't you see I'm far too busy to attend to your whims?'

In Spanish this is known as *atención al cliente*, or 'attention to the client', better known to us as 'customer service'. If the client persists, one is finally duty bound to pay the client attention, however irritating the interruption may be and whatever the nature of the activity one is engaged in at the time. At the supermarkets this would normally be gossiping to the person on the next till or catching up with friends on the cell phone. *Atención al cliente* is one of the exasperating aspects of life in these parts, that can get to people if they're not successful at acclimatising to the culture.

Thankfully, on this occasion, we could limp the short distance home and change cars, but it did mean that we finally rolled up thirty-five minutes and five fateful seconds late, just behind Phil's unmistakable blue van emblazoned with his personal logo. Whoops!

Quickly running through the options in my mind, I decided to act just as I would had it been a coincidence, which it was. The only difference was that I felt really guilty about my tardiness and that his family with him might perceive my hands around the neck of a bag, from which a cat was about to escape and spoil their carefully laid plans.

I took a deep breath and mustered every last dreg of dramatic talent. 'Hello, Phil! What are you doing here?'

'I've come for a birthday party', was his cheery retort. 'What are you doing here?'

That's where I faltered, and before I could stop myself, the words slipped out, 'I thought it was a surprise!'

It didn't matter. Such was the confusion of the moment and the conviction in his mind that it was friend Ken's party he was about to attend rather than his own, that Phil's surprise wasn't threatened in any way. Although his wife, son, and daughter-in-law appeared unconvinced,

Phil remained oblivious to the point that twenty minutes into the proceedings a mutual friend was heard to comment incredulously, 'I don't think Phil quite realises yet this is his party!'

* * * * *

The last Monday in that month was Spring Bank Holiday back in England. Although it was a normal Monday here, that meant our day off, which started with a game of tennis at the Metropolitan Spa. It's hard work keeping afloat financially in sunny Lanzarote, and a generous friend had purchased a year's subscription to enable us to 'take the smooth with the rough'. When Sue wistfully reminded me of the British holiday, my immediate reply was 'It must be tipping it with rain then!' Sure enough, a few minutes later, as I warmed up in the gym, I caught a glimpse of the United Kingdom weather forecast on Sky News. The volume was down but the message was crystal clear. Behind the pretty girl who was in the process of delivering the bad news, huge blue streaks filled the screen, heralding another soggy washout in poor old Blighty! Schadenfreude is mine!

Despite the frequent downpours, we used to make the most of our bank holidays in England. Rain or shine we would be jolly sure to enjoy those precious opportunities to break the routine, get out into the countryside with our two kids in tow and, with great gusto, go about creating the special memories that we are now savouring … Wareham—'Do you remember the Wareham Bears?' Sue asks with a smile and a twinkle in her eyes. Wareham was one of our favourite destinations: the quaint little quay with swans and a cosy little café on the boardwalk, the obligatory teatime outing to the little fish-and-chip shop, the lovely old buildings full of character. And the Wareham Bears! The children loved them and even we were charmed by the cuddly collection of cute furry toys.

Housed in their own special museum (an antiquated little cottage located in the heart of the town) and guarded by a single life-size specimen at the door, the bears occupied two compact, busy floors. It was a wonder to behold as Ali and Jonna's little faces lit up with eager excitement and joy while they lingered over each display in turn. There was a slightly scruffy example of Pooh Bear, which had obviously received a generous portion of loving attention over the years, a more pristine Paddington, looking for all the world as if he'd just arrived fresh from his origins in deepest, darkest Peru, and a rather shabby Rupert hiding shyly in one of the darker corners.

These were just a few of the hundreds of little bears arranged in groups with great care and imagination. One gathering was engaged in a gentle game of cricket, while its neighbours sat quietly enjoying a typically English treat of afternoon tea and cakes. Later, on the phone, I ask Jonna what his abiding memory is of those bygone visits. 'I remember the smell of the place …' That's right; they say that smell is more evocative than any other of our five senses. I immediately recall that same aroma, a unique blend of the slight fustiness of a museum combined with a twist of that comforting furry smell you get as a child when burying your face into the softness of a favourite teddy and inhaling deeply.

Meanwhile, back in Lanzarote, it's time for our regular Monday morning clash on the tennis court. This is our fourth visit to the very smart-looking artificial grass surface, which we approach with rising tension as we emerge from the changing rooms and continue past the spa, up a steadily rising stone-paved corridor, through a doorway to the exterior, and up a steep staircase, set into the hillside, until we emerge rather abruptly, and with some trepidation to face our opponents.

Tyra is a well-spoken English girl of thirty or so years, confident, looks the part in her Wimbledon whites. Caitlin looks older, her skin having borne the brunt of many Australian summers. We are on the other side, but no less well presented—the other side of the netting, that is, not the net.

The first week, Tyra challenged us head on as we hovered hopefully to claim our court, 'Have you booked?'

Yes, we had most definitely booked. Being obedient and helpful members of the Metropolitan Spa, we had duly reserved our slot at main reception, where our name sat neatly inscribed in the reservations book.

Tyra and Caitlin had taken a chance; they always played at this time and had never run into any opposition to the occupation of the hallowed 'turf'. Eventually they abandoned the playing area and graciously allowed us to take up our rightful ownership of the ground, which, in their minds, plainly belonged to them. One, love!

Week two. 'This is ridiculous!' Tyra exclaimed in condescending consternation. Indeed it was.

When will they learn? I wondered. By now our awkward mixture of embarrassment and intimidation was giving way to rising indignation tinged with a certain amount of amusement. But we had to think the best of our worthy opponents, and they were very polite about it after all. Maybe there had been a double booking.

With an alacrity reminiscent of Martina Navratilova running to hit a cross-court forehand winner, Tyra lifted her cell phone and hit a swerving volley to the unsuspecting Susanna up in main reception. 'This is Tyra on the tennis court. I must say I'm very unhappy with this. Look in the book and you can see I play at this time every week!'

In the dizziness induced by this dazzling stroke play, the contradiction took a few seconds to register: last week she'd admitted to not being in the booking habit.

Oh well! Two, love!

So, by week three, our reply to the 'have you booked?' attempt at a backhand winner was as devastating as it was direct. 'Well, actually, I've just come from reception, where I picked up a racquet and four balls and Susanna checked my booking'.

Three, love!

Now it's week four, and we're wondering whether the terrible twosome will be there again. On one hand, it seems unlikely they would persist in the face of the previous weeks' resounding defeats, but on the other, they have made such a strong impression as to have become, in my mind at least, something of a permanent fixture. As we approach the contentious court, I hurry ahead of Sue to find out if we're in for another awkward skirmish across the netting before we get to play the ball-and-racquet variety of tennis that we were always hoping to … unhindered.

A few moments pass before I can fully take in the state of play—'match abandoned', not a soul in sight, just an empty court. But something else is different. Suddenly it hits me; that notice on the gate wasn't there before: 'Dear Guests: The Sports Facilities Must Be Reserved Before Use. Materials Can Be Provided At Reception For Your Convenience. Kind Regards, The Entertainments Team'. Game, set, and match!

Having played and showered, we retire to the salubrious sun terrace of the five-star hotel that plays host to the spa. It's time for lunch, a picnic smuggled in to save the twenty euros I would have been charged at the pool bar.

With the conflict over the use of the tennis court properly behind us, the whole establishment returned to being a proper refuge where we were able to hide away each week and cast off the otherwise-constant burden that accompanies the role of pastor.

*   *   *   *   *

June kicked off with a visit from two of our most delightful friends, who arrived, exhausted but euphoric, after an early start and a night without sleep.

One of the things we hope for on behalf of our guests is that they should make the most of the surprisingly wide range of benefits our little island has to offer. One of these is the beautifully warm, temperate climate. And, at the beginning of June, one of its features is the heralding of the twenty-nine-degree summer months with the strengthening of the prevailing trade winds. It is these that provide perfect conditions for windsurfing, proven by the myriad of colourful craft that cut their swift zigzag paths through the azure blue of the local bays. Their daring acrobatics remind me of demented dancing butterflies with their gossamer like sails jumping, spinning, and bucking over the surface of the sea.

It's funny how you can quickly become accustomed to ten hours a day of sunshine and a refreshing moderate breeze. The onset of the 'windy season' as I termed it apologetically to Zeke and Laura, then appears to us a huge blot on our sunny copybook. But to them, arriving from a wet and windy English spring, it was pure paradise.

We'd known Laura for twenty of her twenty-two years. Her delicate elfin looks fool most new acquaintances into believing she's much younger. As I gave her a big welcoming hug, I got the sensation of having to be careful not to crush her slender frame.

At nearly twenty-one, Ezekiel was a disarmingly open, straight-talking Australian. What you saw as you beheld his well-presented appearance and pleasantly rugged looks that betray his family's Austrian roots, is basically what you got.

They were easy guests. Our son, Jonna, and Zeke were best friends, having been separated since the previous September by Jonna's commencing his university career in the 2008 European capital of culture, the illustrious metropolis of Liverpool. When the hectic schedule of student life screeched to a halt for the long summer vacation, Jonna was looking forward to spending quality time with his closest buddy again. 'Zeke's the only person I can just hang out and be boring with', he confessed.

For Zeke, going easy was an extreme sport, and in that respect he reminded us of our distant son. As we tucked into a delicious evening meal involving tasty salads dressed with balsamic vinegar and treacle and peppered with succulent pieces of fruit, we reminisced affectionately about our absent mate and offspring. There was the time Jonna was found laid out neatly on top of a skip, sending up zeds to the heavens. Admittedly he'd been working with all his customary enthusiasm and energy to fill the container with the remains of a friend's old kitchen wall and was now putting his time waiting for the builder to return to the best use possible, recharging the batteries he'd just drained! We were reminded that we had ample photographic evidence of his impressive ability to precipitate himself into the depths of sleep in the most extraordinary places, one picture in particular testifying to the occasion when at six months old, he nodded off right in the middle of a mouthful of his favourite dish at that age, stewed apple.

The congeniality of Zeke's company is further enhanced by a naive appreciation of all things new and different, such as the spa. 'Prepare to lose a kilo. Have you ever been in the steam room? It's crazy!' At one point we glance across only to see Zeke doing a handstand in the cold Jacuzzi. 'Beautiful isn't it?'

His excitement seemed to strengthen his normal Australian twang still further, 'Sooo narce! Refreshing! Laavely!'

One of the pleasant surprises that our visitors often bring is a new vision of our little island. It never ceases to amaze me how quickly one can come to take for granted even the unique beauty of the extraordinary natural surroundings. So, whenever we played the role of tour guides, it's a new opportunity to go out, get off the beaten track of our daily routine, and look again at those special treasures worthy of fresh discovery.

Our top destination on these infrequent days out is a jewel of a place in the north, unique right down to the species of albino crabs that populate the still, deep lagoon which sits quietly in the semi-darkness of an ancient volcanic crater at the heart of the site. The attraction's name, Jameos del Agua, refers to the volcanic underground chambers that characterise the whole area. Hundreds of these craters, tunnels, and caves were created by a series of powerful volcanic eruptions between three and four thousand years ago, and have since been invaded by the sea and eroded by the elements.

Centred on the flooded cavern with its intriguing little crabs, the tourist attraction was conceived by Cesar Manrique, the *padrón* of Lanzarote art and architecture, who dominated the island culturally during the second half of the twentieth century. Its four levels include a volcano museum, pools, and garden, along with an auditorium, whose construction completed work on the site in 1987. Among the dark volcanic stone terraces, linked by rocky staircases, there are all sorts of fascinating little corners. In this fusion of powerful natural forces and the artist's creative genius, it's not just his vision that's staggering. One has to marvel equally at the extraordinary feat of engineering that turned thousands of tons of volcanic rock into this surprising hideaway.

The first terrace on the way down to the lagoon serves as a coffee bar. It perches on a wide ledge, halfway down the wall of the deep crater. As one looks up to the sky, the floor recedes into a cave, with a long bar towards the back. A visit to the toilets takes one further in. These bathrooms are housed in more caves, and yet further small caverns can be seen, lit up beyond. The average tourist, leaving the coach for a quick whirl around, hasn't enough time to take advantage of the calming peacefulness offered by this first terrace. On less hurried visits, we've tarried over a cup of coffee and a book for hours here, the haunting mood music that plays quietly in the background adding to the tranquil sense of otherworldliness.

A rocky stairway links this first stage with the lowest part of the complex. As it winds the visitor down to the cool, dark cavern housing the subterranean lagoon, each broad step is a jigsaw of dark volcanic rock pieces. Shiny green ferns stand watching silently from the rocky slopes, while giant Swiss cheese plants sprawl their way up towards the light. Arriving at the edge of the water and looking across to the shadowy terrace and sunlit slopes on the far side of the cave, one gets the impression of looking into a distant mirror.

Manrique was a master of detail. Square volcanic rock balustrades act as railings along the balcony that creates a solid path along the right-hand wall of the cave. As casual tourists stop to peer into the depths, they probably don't notice the rugged craftwork of these structures, as their attention is drawn inexorably to the hundreds of bright little crabs that inhabit the deep, each one no larger than a fingernail. Neither are they likely to be aware of the way that he has picked out individual outcrops behind them, surrounding them in big flashes of white paint reminiscent of the explosions, now frozen in time, that brought forth the fantastic rockscape. Where he has painted over the uneven parts, the white knobbly surface remind me of rocky road ice cream.

Emerging slowly into the sunshine through a volcanic pergola and on to the next terrace, the main theme is a white satin finish, starting with the final few steps which resemble railway sleepers set into the smooth white painted rock. The centrepiece of this sunken garden is a huge kidney-shaped swimming pool, whose pristinely white sides slope into deep turquoise water reflecting the colour of the sky above. Completing the sense of tropical luxury is a bending coconut palm, which spreads its canopy high above the water's surface.

The auditorium, tucked away inauspiciously in the far corner, is worthy of marvel in its own right. Manrique has managed his usual blend of nature and art to convert a huge cavern into an extraordinary underground amphitheatre.

Volcanic rock steps introduce the visitor to the final level, paved again with the ubiquitous rock. Here the volcanic pillars take natural forms, reflecting the geology of the caves below, and are embellished with ferns sprouting out all around. A second opportunity for a cup of coffee or *refresco* (cold drink) is one I've never been known to miss, reluctant as I always am to leave for the next stop on the tour.

CHAPTER 10

Mad Dogs and Englishmen

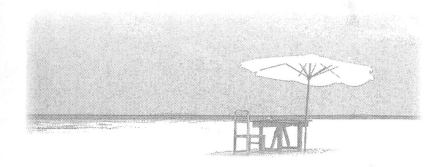

BEFORE ZEKE AND LAURA left us, we all trooped off to one of the loveliest beaches on the island. What better time to choose for a church barbecue than the exact hour when the fierce Lanzarote sun is at its highest all year, two p.m. on the twenty-second of June? As we arrived at our traditional spot on the seawater lagoon at the most unspoiled, beautiful white sandy beach on Lanzarote, it was easy to spot the Brits. The Spaniards were the ones camping in large family groups under huge awnings covering great, living room-size squares of sand in cool obscurity, while the northern Europeans sat on the sand, baking in the sun like washed-up crabs.

At church a fortnight earlier, we'd all been marvelling at the perfect geometrical shape and deep, even red colour of the skin covering the lowest quarter of the back of one of our ladies, Gerie. She had inadvertently exposed the gap between the bottom of her T-shirt and top of her trousers to the sun, while attending to the abundance of low growing unwanted plants in her ample back garden.

To cap that, as we met for worship that morning, she had even been showing off a new swathe of siren-red sunburn, extending from her shoulders to halfway down her spine. 'I can't understand it', she said. 'In all my nine years living here, that's never happened to me, and now I go and burn myself twice in two weeks!' One awestruck visitor was even heard to comment, 'That's third degree, isn't it?'

As for me, when it comes to the sun, I'm usually extremely careful. Since living here, accompanying a number of people to interpret at the oversubscribed skin clinic at Arrecife hospital has left an indelible impression on my mind. I've watched one patient after another being examined by the consultant dermatologist and explained to them on his behalf the extent of the damage they have done to themselves by prolonged and repeated exposure to the penetrating solar rays that beat down on our vulnerable skin 338 days of every Lanzarote year.

It's always the same place that is affected, although that's not on the back where Gerie caught it. Rather, it is that V-neck portion around the collarbone that is always open to the day star's penetrating gaze. The effect reminds me of the red volcanic landscape of Timanfaya National Park. Precancerous pustules erupt from deep within the lowest layers of the largest organ of the body, where previously healthy tissue has been turned into a volatile cauldron.

Accordingly, as soon as Sue and I had finished the morning's business of catching up with our church family on various matters and putting away all the bits and pieces to do with the multimedia systems that have become an essential part of modern church meetings, we repaired to the bathroom to apply liberal amounts of protective cream, before venturing into the furnace.

Approaching the beach at La Santa for the first time is an

interesting experience. First, one has to negotiate the village, with its wide central street spanned by humongous great blue-and-white-striped sleeping policemen who 'calm' the traffic to a leisurely crawl. Leaving the restaurants, cafés, and water-sport shops behind, the road takes on the dimensions of an airstrip, as it leads gently downhill towards its terminus, Club La Santa, a grand complex that provides training for world-renowned sportspeople alongside family sporting holidays. Sitting there in splendid isolation, a vast arrangement of white tubular turrets and rectangular blocks, it reminds me of something out of *2001: A Space Odyssey*.

In my imagination, the mysterious palace crowns the end of an ancient desert highway. Aliens landed here several millennia ago and established it as their first terrestrial colony. Now and again there emerge a little bevy of the strange hybrid creatures that must have resulted from their mingling with a lost race of primitive hominids. Their crustaceous skulls are streamlined and shiny, their bug eyes dark yet gleaming, and their stooped forms hunched forward, as they sweep along the road, reclaiming their ancestral right of way. I call them the *Psi-clysts*.

In fact, the whole island is a popular training ground for cyclists, who seem to appreciate the challenge as much as the astounding beauty offered by the rolling terrain, especially in the ideal conditions offered by the warm, dry winter weather. The presence of a peloton blocking the carriageway can be an irritation to resident drivers like myself. But then I just have to adjust my view, regard it as an invitation to slow down to a proper Lanzarote pace, and enjoy a gentle cruise through the spectacular scenery that draws them here.

Halfway along the lugubrious approach road to the La Santa sports complex, on the left-hand side, is a single, large white house that stands like a sentry guarding the lagoon beyond. Turning left, we rattle and shudder our way over the barely made road along the curve of the bay, and finally peel off down one of the short sandy tracks onto the broad sea wall that encloses a kilometre of quiet seaside bliss.

As we joined our little gang on the sand and looked out over the water, I couldn't help being reminded of the boating lake I used to frequent as a child. It was there I learned how to fall out of a ten foot Moth sailing dinghy. Actually, I'm lying; falling out was the most natural thing in the world. What I had to learn was how to clamber back in and turn the capsized boat back on its keel. As the odd windsurfer and pair of canoeists completed the scene, the sailing theme was reinforced. Nevertheless, the overall impression was of chill-out zone, with many local people parked up in an assortment of temporary homes, from simple tents to caravans and top-of-the-range convertible RVs. The local tradition is to move out of home for the summer and spend the whole season living on the beach. If you had nine weeks holiday entitlement as standard, what would you do?

Having arrived, we unpacked the charcoal, and Ray was able to go about the business of cooking up a tasty barbecue. The first food to hit the grill was in the form of the fat, pink pork sausages that are regularly consumed here with great relish. As well as being full of flavour, they are, unlike English sausages, full of meat! Then there were some beautiful pieces of juicy steak. I'm always staggered at the way the food seems to multiply on these occasions. It's like the feeding of the five thousand! The evening before, we had feasted with our good friends Denis and Marika to such an extent that I hadn't needed any breakfast that morning. This meant that I had plenty of room for the bumper barbecue. Then somebody produced some beautifully cooked, succulent panga, one of the more economical forms of white fish available to us here. Its delicate flavour was further enhanced by an interesting sauce purchased *günstig*, as the Germans would say, at a bargain price, from the German supermarket situated just below our church premises. The shop had been a convenient source of cheap and tasty wines, sauces, and other drinks, ever since it opened a few months previously. It was at this point that my abundant appetite gave out.

Finally, sometime later, the chicken that had been cooking slowly and thoroughly over a prolonged period was declared fit and ready for our consumption. By then, however, nobody wanted to eat ever again. I felt really sorry for poor old Ray, who had been tending the grill with near infinite patience and care for the last three and a half hours!

Ray is not just a master barbecue chef, he is a walking miracle of medical science. As we watched the sausages sizzle while we fried ourselves in the warm sunshine, he filled me in on all the gory details. He told me how he had been admitted to hospital in Las Palmas with severe headaches and a tiny lump above his right eye. He was about to undergo an enema when his cell phone rang; it was his sister. As soon as he told her what was happening, she realised from her experience in nursing that the hospital was giving him a treatment that was utterly inappropriate to his condition. 'Get out of there now, get on a plane, and come back to England!' she ordered. His illness turned out to be a cancerous tumour. By the time he had complied with his sister's behest, got back to the United Kingdom, and been attended by some of the most skilful surgeons of the realm, he was only a few days from being inoperable. Having removed the top right-hand quarter of his skull and taken away the tumours, they reconstructed his head using tissue taken from other parts of his body, including a big wadge of muscle from his leg. The hazardous procedure lasted nearly twenty-four hours, was without precedent, and has never been attempted since.

In addition to saving his life, they were able to preserve his right eye and ear, which had both been under threat. According to Ray, they even improved his looks! The lack of hair on the right-hand portion of his scalp is normally covered by a stylishly worn cowboy hat. The brim and front of the hat tilted downward a tad, combined with his newly angled eyebrow, creates an engaging Western look that perfectly suits his lively character.

Two years on, Ray was keen to pass on a message of encouragement to other cancer sufferers. Consulting with his Macmillan nurse, she had advised him he wasn't yet ready; he was only just coming to terms with the magnitude of the events that have overtaken him. For the whole church, it's a great encouragement every time we see Ray, reminding us of how powerfully God can answer our prayers through the wonderful work of surgeons, doctors, and nurses.

Ray and Paula are an inspiration, not just in the way they've battled against the odds and are still here to tell the tale. Having looked death full in the face, they know what matters in life. In the world that, even in laid-back Lanzarote, is full of worry and hurry, they encourage us to stop our fearful fretting about the future, pause for a moment, look around at the present, and appreciate the gifts of life, love, and friendship that we all have the privilege of sharing in.

Friendship was what our little barbecue was all about, as we sat in the sun together, sharing one another's company and simply enjoying being there. As the water receded, it left us with a soggy three-a-side soccer pitch, just perfect for the game that ensued. These family soccer games are always a bit uneven, and it's almost as much as I can do to avoid treading on some of the smaller children. To add to the fun, we were joined by an enthusiastic and surprisingly skilled little dog, who was immediately christened 'littl'un' by one of the lads. Through an artful combination of wild, carefree play and the odd piece of skill, we managed to keep the score level pegging.

Finally, as my less committed team-mates wandered off, I found myself in a climactic one-on-one with six-year-old Gracie. As she ran around me in rings and finally booted the ball past me with the awkward daintiness of a little princess, bisecting perfectly the imaginary goal line between the two gouges we'd made in the wet sand, I was left wondering whether I had deliberately allowed her to win or my soccer skills had really deteriorated to a level below that of my determined young opponent. I consoled myself by noting how easily I'd overcome my competitive instincts and allowed her the happiness of having her day on the beach crowned with a sporting victory.

Sadly, the atmosphere between the Spanish-speaking churches was not nearly so friendly. Hugo was the latest to break his ties with pastor Santiago, (or Santiago Santiago Santiago, to give him his full name), who had planted all of those churches and had been overseeing them, as well as our own. I was so disappointed! I had been looking forward to working closely with my neighbour and fellow pastor, ever since the Festival for the Family four years previously. My visit to his church had been the climax of the week for me personally. He had invited me to preach, which I considered a great privilege. I had never used my Spanish language that way before, so it was with trepidation and excitement that I drove down to Playa Blanca for the occasion. I was flying high emotionally and spiritually, and I'll never forget singing along to the song 'Eagle's Wings' by Hillsong as I headed along the new, unfamiliar road from Yaiza down to the coastal resort. Every time I hear it now, I can still see myself on the final stretch of the bypass and remember the feeling of elation and anticipation.

Having delivered my sermon successfully, another challenge immediately reared its ugly head. I was invited to join Hugo in praying over individuals in the substantial crowd of worshippers who had come forward with the different needs for healing. I approached each individual, asked them what they wanted, and duly prayed. I could see people to my right keeling over, as Hugo's prayers were bringing them under the power of the Holy Spirit. My own prayers had never had that effect, so I felt under pressure to see my own people go down.

'Look', I counselled myself, 'it doesn't matter. Just look to God and ask him to do his stuff'. As I let go of the anxiety and just focussed on appealing to him, I was relieved to see the next person crumple and succumb physically to God's power!

*　　*　　*　　*　　*

When I first arrived in these foreign parts, I was so completely determined to put my homeland behind me that I mentally branded all things English as bad. It's not easy to leave the country of one's birth, childhood, and even thirty years of adulthood. Besides, there are some very good things about England, and one of those, which is appreciated greatly by people from all over the globe, is the traditional English breakfast.

So, two years and four months into our new life in the sun, you can imagine my delight at the suggestion of Pastor Charlie that our next pastors' meeting should start at 9.00 a.m. Straight away I volunteered to supply the food, fully confident that a hearty English breakfast would provide the perfect gourmet start to our monthly get-together. Paul would do a wonderful job, and the church café was the perfect setting.

Succulent images of tasty sizzling sausages, fried eggs with luscious yellow yolks sitting on soft whites, flavoursome rashers of pink bacon caramelised with a sheen of brown, big red, juicy tomatoes, and a clutch of button mushrooms freshly fried in butter sprang to mind.

Now, one has to take the utmost care in cross-cultural situations such as ours. Even between Canarians, Colombians, and other Spanish speakers, there can be misunderstandings, despite their common language. And so it is that the word 'breakfast' translates exactly and unequivocally to *desayuno* in Spanish. An *ayuno* is a fast, so a *desayuno* is a break of the fast. However, the concept of a generous meal at the start of the day, to someone of Spanish extraction, is entirely foreign. *Desayuno* for them is more a mid-morning snack, eaten on the Hispanic hoof. Serious eating is reserved for 'lunchtime', which is mid-afternoon to us. This feast commences generally between the hours of 2.00 and 4.00 p.m. and is followed traditionally by the famous siesta.

For this reason, it was with a certain surprise and lack of readiness that my Hispanic colleagues reacted when they rolled up nonchalantly between 9.00 and 9.30 on the appointed morning. 'So we're starting with breakfast?' Charlie asked incredulously.

'That's right', I replied, as the anticipation of a hearty breakfast and keen feelings of hunger gave way to a sinking feeling in the pit of my stomach.

Finally, on the dot of 9.45 a.m., Santiago opened the proceedings: 'Let's eat!'

Okay, now we're talking! I thought, somewhat relieved. I don't really know what revived my spirits—it may have been the nutritious meal or the distraction of carefully combining the elements on my plate so that the creamy yolk complemented perfectly the tanginess of the bacon, and the sweetness of the tomato coordinated precisely with the herbiness of the carefully sliced sausages. It could equally have been the high caffeine content of my mug of coffee.

However, I found my friends' initial reaction a bit of a disappointment. They all went rather quiet. Then one of them commented incredulously, 'Is this what you eat every day? It's very high in protein!'

It wasn't until a few minutes after the meal had ended that my friends started to give me more positive feedback about the food that was now evidently having its beneficial effects upon them. '¡*Fenomenal!*' ('Very good!') '¡*Muchisimas gracias!*' ('Thank you very much!') I concluded that, the human organism being a finely tuned and closely adjusted piece of machinery, foreigners, unaccustomed to the digestion of English food, must take a bit longer to release energy from the unfamiliar nutrients and register the effect in the brain.

In reality, my friends were very gracious and speedy in their adaptation to the timing and content of our breakfast, much more than the average Brit abroad in taking up the local customs, above all when it comes to eating and the hours we keep. Of course, nutritionally, we expats are constrained by what's available. In our part of the world, the shops don't stock a wide range of foodstuffs, and English tastes are not completely catered for. When English foods are on sale, then inevitably the prices reflect their exceptional nature.

Normally the monthly pastors' meeting starts somewhat later, at eleven, which means the accompanying meal is what we would call 'lunch' and is taken after the proceedings rather than before. It also means the character of the meal is that of a feast. The absence of a proper breakfast from the Hispanic diet also has implications. From the moment we begin, the table is piled with plates of crisps, nuts, and other nibbles, and the meeting is conducted to the background noise of constant munching.

I always start well, understanding everything that's said. The prayers are clear and formulated in language that is familiar to my ears. Pastor Santiago's address, based on a passage from the Bible, is always delivered clearly in his breathy accent that is so typical of educated Canarians. However, as soon as the other pastors chip in, I'm lost. The thing is that, without exception, all five are Colombian. I simply wasn't used to not being able to follow spoken Spanish and couldn't work out why. With the Canarians, the subject is quite straightforward. They are mostly country people of little education. When tourism came to the island a generation ago, they became rich overnight, selling the land or building hotels and shopping complexes and making a mint by letting them out to rich foreigners. The need for education bypassed them completely. This has left them speaking, as I suspect country people speak the world over, with a broad accent and a simplified grammar. That's why I find those who speak with a heavier accent borders on incomprehensible.

One day, as I was sitting in Santiago's office for one of our regular monthly meetings, and opening my heart to him, I asked, 'Why is it that I just can't understand the Colombians?'

The pastor's response was simple: 'It's sheer velocity!'

Ah! I thought, *That must be it; Santiago should know if anybody does.*

Having said that, I'm still not convinced. Perhaps I'll have worked it out by the time I write my next book.

As Santiago looked around the café, he asked how business was going. I had to admit Cathy and her crew were starting to struggle. The whole island was quiet, a phenomenon we all put down to the recent strengthening of the euro. When we had been purchasing a house a year previously, we had been able to buy each euro for seventy pence or less. Now tourists from the United Kingdom were having to pay ninety pence, adding nearly a third to their holiday expenses.

On top of that, we were discovering that the previous business, Caca Milis, had found a niche into which ours was never going to fit. The Irish cake and coffee shop was well known in the Republic, having even been the subject of a TV documentary. Prospective customers were turning away when they found the old incumbents were no longer trading.

*   *   *   *   *

As if the troubles with the church café weren't enough, our home was now invaded by the most difficult of guests. Whereas it is normally one of the joys of life on a holiday island to receive visitors, having this couple to stay is something else! Friends and family often combine the opportunity of taking a break in the sun with the joy of being reunited with, and catching up with us. It's always lovely to see them arrive. As we wait expectantly for them to emerge through the sliding doors in the busy arrivals hall of Arrecife airport, there's all the anticipation of several days, or sometimes several weeks, of their presence with us.

And when they finally go, as we watch them negotiate their way through the ever-stricter security checks and eventually cross the line into the spacious departure lounge beyond, we always turn towards our empty home with a mixture of sadness, satisfaction, and, sometimes, relief, according to the particular nature of our relationship.

The problem with Angela is simple; Angela argues. You can't actually *tell* her anything. She knows it all already, so there's really no point. Of course, I knew this and have known it for, well, ever since I've had the very mixed pleasure of knowing her. But it's easy to forget. In order to make things easier during these unsolicited visits, we got into the useful habit of putting on one of our many DVDs to pass the evenings more agreeably, literally to avoid the disagreements between Angela and whomever she may be addressing at any given moment.

So, at the end of *Bombon el Perro* (*Bombon the Dog*), a particularly enjoyable film, in the euphoria of the moment I forgot myself and started to share enthusiastically the things I'd learned about the making of the film from the bonus material. I've always found the subject of filmmaking fascinating, and on this occasion, the thing that fired my imagination and enthusiasm about this beautifully related story of a man and his randomly acquired canine companion was the way the director had used ordinary people as actors and simply told them to play themselves. So, for example, the leading role of the amiable Coco Vargas is played by the very same Coco Vargas. What a joy it must be to play yourself in an enchanting story some screenwriter has made up for you!

Anyway, my inability to contain my enthusiasm was castigated swiftly and effectively with a dismissive, 'Well, of course, all directors are doing that now!'

That was news to me! There must be a lot of out-of-work actors around! But there's absolutely no point whatsoever in responding to Angela with logic. Her perception of the world is so different from reality that effectively she is living on another planet.

I will spare you from the full extent of the pain these visits cause us. However, if you'll allow me to indulge myself and offload just one more aspect of these admittedly infrequent but nonetheless outrageous interruptions of our idyllic existence, then probably the most uncomfortable feature is the constant bickering between Angela and her partner Greg. At breakfast once, I just happened to mention an item of news. Unlike most Brits we have no English-language TV, and so I consider it polite, if not my bounden duty, to keep guests up to date with important developments in the affairs of the world. So when there was a giant Lego man mysteriously washed up on a Dutch beach, of course I informed Angela and Greg of the intriguing incident. I hadn't counted on the danger of invoking Angela's expert knowledge about the rate of rise in the level of the North Sea, and above all, I hadn't foreseen the hot debate that would be unleashed by my merely passing on an inconsequential item of news. Thankfully I was just finishing my kiwi fruit, which customarily constitutes the final course of my first meal of the day, and I was able to make a quick escape with my dirty plate and bowl to the dishwasher.

Twenty minutes later, Sue and I having sat down to our 9.00 a.m. Tuesday planning meeting, I popped out to get a drink, and it was all I could do to keep myself from bursting with laughter. I just managed to make it back to the office with my dignity intact. The pair of them were still deep in the same ridiculous debate!

There is one last lesson I have learned from my dealings with this extraordinary couple. Even if it does not benefit my readers, perhaps it will serve to help myself remember for next year. Angela can, and will, pick fault with any information I may venture. The only safe ground is to simply relate an experience I have had that she cannot lay claim to herself—even she can't argue about those!

Thankfully we were able to get Denis and Marika around for an evening, thus giving us a break from Angela and Greg's unrelenting company. This proved to be the greatest test of Denis's conversational skills, and one he passed with flying colours. I had to be really careful not to let my jaw drop too noticeably as the two of them chatted away. Not that they would have noticed anyway!

Another means of escape was the spa. It had become quite a haven for us, quickly attaining the status of a second home. As our contentious guests continued to occupy our home, we presented ourselves to Pilar, one of the friendly girls at the spa reception. 'We're escaping our visitors. It's because of them that we've not been able to come the last week!' 'Oh well, that's the price of living in Lanzarote!' reflected Pilar philosophically.

As we stepped into our bolt hole with a great sigh of relief, I recalled how at first the pool area had felt so new and wonderful. The large stone chamber is reminiscent of an ancient palace with its colonnades, and extensive system of luxurious pools, showers, suites, and terraces. As the warm scented air embraces the new arrival, attendants floating around silently in their oriental white garb complete the regal atmosphere. The wide eyes of hotel guests as they tread its hallowed precincts bear witness to the depth of its first impression.

After a while, of course, we had found ourselves travelling the same old path on every visit. Leaving the changing room to deposit our towels on poolside bed, we would lower ourselves into the main pool and then work our way through our favourite jets, giving ourselves a watery massage of the same muscles, in the same order. As one French lady I swapped remarks with said one time, *'On s'y habitue—vite et bien!'* ('You soon become accustomed to it—and well accustomed at that!') Nevertheless, it was a comfortable familiarity, and the place still served as a great escape where we allowed the burdens to roll off our shoulders as they succumbed to the warm flow.

Since our confrontation with Tyra and Caitlin over the booking of the tennis court and the resultant posting of the sign requesting people to book, further signs had gone up around the facilities, each one obviously signalling the perpetration of yet another class of persistent misdemeanour. It seems that these days even the users of five-star hotels often lack the common decency one would normally expect of them. Such people the Spanish call *sin vergüenzas* ('people without shame')—those who show a brazen lack of respect for those around them.

The next lot of *sin vergüenzas* to provoke the production of a notice was a rather too jolly group of Spanish speakers, led by a very large man whose appearance put me in mind of some Egyptian eunuch from a 1960s film. I first became aware of his presence when I tried to use the changing room one afternoon. The facility usually becomes rather crowded when the third male spa user arrives. This man was capable of, and indeed could not avoid, making it impassable on his own. In fact, he apologised, and I quickly exited backward through the entrance I had just used.

Unfortunately, the volume of his voice matched his size, and the rest of his family was as loud and large. The girls on the desk were in quite a quandary. The man and his family wouldn't listen to their remonstrations, and even their usually forthright boss, whom we had nicknamed 'Madame', seemed to be at a loss. 'They're not even hotel guests!' she confided in me. 'I've told the girls to refuse if they try to book again'. That was the last we saw of them. There swiftly followed the posting of another notice, *'Please keep the silence!'*

Thankfully we weren't witnesses to the next infringement. As we passed the hot room one morning, a new notice had been posted on the door: *'Costumes must be worn in the sauna'.*

I often speculate with Sue what the next notice to go up might be. As well as enjoying the spa ourselves, it can be fun to observe those around us. The relaxing effect of lying in the warm water and being massaged by the different jets is really quite extraordinary. As people unwind, it often leads to a certain amount of laughter and playful behaviour. Each person reacts in their own way. Personally, I prefer to simply flop like a raggedy doll and allow my facial features to fall naturally into an inane grin.

The Jacuzzi seats four people comfortably but is more usually taken by a couple. It's warm bubbling water lends itself to the exchange of the odd affectionate caress under the surface. But some couples seem to lose all sense of self-consciousness and can be seen canoodling with complete abandon. As Sue was remarking on the intimate nature of one particular pair's embrace one day, I joked, 'You know the next sign that will go up, don't you? *No sex in the Jacuzzi!*'

They say it takes all sorts, and we certainly have found that to be equally true when it comes to spa users as well as to our guests and the way they behave in our home. Thankfully we don't have to play Hotel Herman too often, and I guess it helps us appreciate the peace and quiet that we normally enjoy in both of these havens.

* * * * *

By June, the church café was in dire straits. Paul and Cathy couldn't even afford to pay themselves, let alone Sue. The offer of work from the wedding organisers came to nothing, and other work promised by friends similarly failed to materialise. Job advertisements were virtually non-existent. Finally Sue was given a day's cleaning at a villa, resulting in painful tennis elbow, which left her with continual pain for months afterward! Then, at the end of June, there suddenly appeared an advertisement for a very appropriate position at a local resort, and Sue responded. She was called for interview the day before we were due to join our friends on holiday in France. As I sat waiting in one corner of the complex, I took the opportunity to enjoy the lengthy article and pictures in the national daily *El País* covering the previous day's epic Wimbledon final between Rafael Nadal and Roger Federer. I was just savouring the delightful description under the heading *Nadal Conquista Wimbledon* (Nadal Conquers Wimbledon) when a text message came in from Cathy asking me to call. Paul had finally walked out. I consoled her the best I could, but I think we both knew at that point her dream was over.

Sue finally emerged from a long interview looking very confident, with the promise that the management would phone the next day, hopefully, to confirm her appointment. Her potential lady boss was very pleasant and they immediately hit it off. It looked like the answer to Sue's prayers. The position she was going for involved making sure that the resort's users simply had a good holiday and would want to return—something Sue was eminently suited to with her recent experience in tourism and her winsome character.

The following morning, as we woke to the five a.m. alarm, we started our journey to join our friends and neighbours, David and Liz, for a week on the canals of Burgundy, France.

David and Liz are what we call 'swallows'. They overwinter in Lanzarote and fly north in the spring to spend the warmer months in cooler climes. David is an engineer. Not that he spent his working life in strictly that field. He met Liz while they were both working in newly independent Zambia, he in public health and she in the foreign office. Prior to retirement, they ran a well-oiled narrow-boat business on the Monmouthshire and Brecon Canal, fondly known as the 'Mon and Brec' to its friends, that runs through the green hills and well-watered Usk Valley of South Wales. David is an expert in engineering in relation to water in particular. He cleverly adapted their fleet of canal-going cruisers, using the water that takes the heat from the engine to feed the radiators which bring essential warmth to the chillier days of the season.

Since those business days he has designed and fitted out their own canal going vessel for the purpose of spending as long as the season allows floating gently through the peaceful pastures of the fat Burgundy countryside. The boat was christened the *Mornington Croissant*, a play on words, based on the title of a favourite comedy radio show, *Mornington Crescent*. Among friends, it was referred to simply as *The Bateau*. David had cleverly adapted an 'off the shelf' layout; cutting back areas of unnecessary steelwork in the bulky frame, he had managed to create more space inside, allowing its crew an unrestricted view from the living room and free access to the kitchen, which lay forward and down a couple of steps. In short, David is a mechanical mastermind. He is also very kind and has been known to rescue our swimming pool from the combined effects of my rather less well-engineered attentions and the lack of a cover.

Liz is a wonderfully attentive and thoughtful hostess. She soon learns her regular guests' favourite drinks, and presents us unfailingly with delicious dishes that the likes of Nigella Lawson and Delia Smith would be proud of.

In principle, the journey was reasonably straightforward: EasyJet to Madrid, then a connecting flight to Paris, followed by a train ride across the French capital, with the final leg being another rail trip through the countryside and down to the heart of beautiful Burgundy. Thankfully there were no delays, just a few queues and a lot of sitting around. Finally we arrived around nine p.m. at Montbard to a warm welcome from our hosts.

The first morning after our arrival, Liz was quick off the mark. As soon as I hit the poop deck, where the captain sits at the wheel at the back of the boat and the guests gather to view the passing pastures, she was offering the first coffee of the day: 'I've put the kettle on. Would you like me to go down and fix you a coffee?'

'I've had one, thank you! Otherwise I'd be incapable of speech', I replied.

Liz was surprised. 'It's that important, is it?'

It was indeed. I'd already hit the mark, having plotted the coordinates for the mug, grains, and hot water into my autopilot the night before.

A few minutes later, she was calling up from the lower quarters again: 'Would Chris like a fruit salad?'

David was in the captain's seat, ready to relay the latest offer, 'Sorry, are you talking to me, love? Fruit salad, Christopher?'

'Oh, yes please!'

'The answer is yes, please'.

A wonderful riot of juicy colours and flavours was duly presented. I approved straight away. 'Mmm, this is a wonderful fruit salad!'

'It is good, isn't it? She does a good 'un!' David agreed.

The mango spurred me to recount immediately and with a chuckle our recent experience at an Indian restaurant back home in Spain.

'Sue's chicken curry arrived with a great relish, but to her surprise, and great disappointment, I might add, unaccompanied by the customary mango chutney! Can you believe that? Anyway, it transpired that neither the waitress nor the chef had ever heard of *el chutney de mango*. So we attempted to explain! In the end, she scuttled off and returned a few moments later with an offering of three little brass bowls, each filled with a different sauce. The red one turned out to be strawberry jam, which actually went very nicely with my Bombay Lamb, the green was mint sauce, again very nice with the lamb, and the brown one livened up Sue's chicken. When she came back, we hadn't the heart to say none of them was the chutney. We just expressed our approval and wondered at the mystery of the mango chutney!'

That first day saw an early start.

'Au revoir, Montbard', I said.

David was reminded of a humorous quote from another favourite radio comedy. 'Yes. Good-bye Montbard, or is it "au revoir, Smithers"? *Beyond The Fringe*,' he continued. 'They had a silly sketch. I think Jonathan Miller was one of them and Peter Cook. The commanding officer issues the order, "Now look here, Smithers, we've reached the stage in the war where we need to send someone over there on a futile gesture. I want you to get up in a crate, pop over to Bremen, take a shufti, don't come back! Okay?" Basically he's saying b-gger off—some pointless gesture, you see'.

Then he came to Smithers's response: 'So Smithers says, "Well, good-bye, sir, or is it au revoir?" and the answer is firmly, "*No*, Smithers!"'

I burst into laughter at David's comic emphasis.

'It was that "*No*, Smithers"; it's not au revoir, it *is* good-bye', David continued as he dissolved into hearty laughter and snorting, finishing with a nostalgic reflection, 'Those silly lines! *Beyond the Fringe*, yes'.

Having completed the morning leg of the day's cruise, Liz rustled up another wonderful offering of sandwiches a la Française. 'Mmm, that pâté de campagne is gorgeous!' she commented as we all tucked in.

'It's a good 'un, love—good butties! Well buttificated!' David added.

'Beautiful!' I chimed in.

Sue was checking her cell phone again for any missed calls from her potential employer. It was difficult for her to relax; she was desperate for work, and this post seemed ideal. Nonetheless, in David and Liz's eminently capable and highly hospitable hands, we continued to enjoy the best of what France has to offer, as we plied our gentle way along the quiet waterways.

As the Spanish would say, the weather accompanied us during our three days' cruising. The warm, dry conditions, with a nice splash of sunshine now and again, permitted us to sit back on the poop deck alongside our captain. As David navigated carefully the sometimes-shallow, and in places very narrow, waterways, we were transfixed by the beautiful scenery that slipped by gently on both sides of *The Bateau*, constantly opening new vistas before us.

As we polished off our fruit salad before setting out on day two, David said, 'That's interesting! There's a dead tree, with dead mistletoe on it. So when the host dies, the parasite dies too'.

'Did the mistletoe kill the tree, then?' I inquired.

'Well, a heavily infested tree is probably less vigorous than it would be. I don't know if it killed it; but certainly that tree's died for whatever reason, and the jolly old mistletoe has died as well'. He paused for a moment and finished with a swish of his characteristic humour. 'That'll teach it!' he chuckled.

'Those are foxgloves, are they? Those purply things'. I was pointing to some flowers on the right, growing below us beside the water.

David rattled off a long Latin name, of which I just managed to catch the final syllable 'Epilobium angustifolium, I think. That's the Latin for them; my grandfather taught me the name of those. I don't think they're foxgloves'.

'No, foxgloves would bear the same name as the poison, digitalis, wouldn't they?' I recalled.

'That's right; it's not foxgloves. It's a clever little flower, grows by the roadside or in the ballast by a railway track—epilobium angustifolium'.

I still didn't catch the name. 'You said that nearly as quickly as you said Llanfairpwllgwyn …!' I exclaimed, recalling about the first tenth of the longest place name in Wales. David had been reminding us the night before that the railway station sign is longer than the platform.

'Well, if you've got it, flaunt it, that's what I say!' David finished with the usual humour. We chuckled together again.

Each day we set out purposefully following a leisurely breakfast including the obligatory croissants—perfectly baked with a delicate crust of golden brown. Lunchtime and dinnertime saw Liz conjuring up one more tasty dish after another, her excellent choice of fresh local produce accompanied by equally flavoursome glasses of French wine.

It was only as we approached our destination, the pretty little town of Clamecy, that there were any signs of the weather breaking. The medieval town was a great place to tie up, with all its holiday amenities, restaurants, and local market, as well as the river and canal with all their interesting comings and goings. The plan was to be there in time to claim a good mooring spot from which to view the fireworks of the fourteenth of July. This allowed us three days there to take advantage of all the place had to offer, including more festivities on Bastille Day.

As we waited, I would sit listening with close attention and great pleasure to the ball by ball commentary of the latest cricket test match between England and South Africa. Liz is an avid cricket fan, while for me it was refreshing to be able to listen to a sport that I had always enjoyed, but had not had the means to tune in to for a couple of years. The clash between the two nations had been greatly anticipated. South Africa were riding high, unbeaten in contests with some of the greatest cricketing countries over the previous season in the southern hemisphere. The fierce attack of their fast bowlers was feared the world over. So it was very uplifting to hear Kevin Pietersen amassing a score of 152 runs, and our whole team notching up just seven runs short of 600 in the first two days, with the magnificent Bell finishing on 199. The only disappointment was that our bowlers, having dismissed the South Africans for half our own score, were unable to follow through, with the match fizzling out to a draw on a flattening wicket.

The great annual firework display promised to be far from a fizzle. As we looked forward to it, we had great fun watching the traditional local water jousting. The practice of balancing precariously on a floating wooden structure is said to date back half a millennium to a time when France's capital city started consuming more wood to keep itself warm and fed than it could provide for itself. The solution was to steer flotillas of logs down the river Yonne, starting at Clamecy, precipitating the town to fame, along with the odd raftsman into its waters. Hence the competition to see who can stay atop the raft the longest. The winner is crowned the *Roi Sec*, the Dry King, that is the last contestant left standing on the prow of his specially adapted rowing boat, waving triumphantly a sort of giant cotton bud that serves as a lance.

After two days of jousting and other jollification, it was time for the climactic fireworks. From the morning onwards the expectation built around the town quay, as the crew arrived with all the pyrotechnic material and assembled the structures needed to support it. Finally, at eleven p.m., the long-awaited moment came. The first fuse was lit and the quayside exploded into a twenty-minute spectacle of light, colour, and loud explosions, filling the night sky overhead and giving me the sensation of being bombarded in the same way as the notorious Bastille more than two hundred years previously. Reflecting on the day's amusement, I couldn't help but note the irony of finding myself, a comfortable middle-class Englishman, being entertained by these peculiar rituals all stemming from the pitiful plight of the poor shivering peasants of Paris in bygone generations.

*   *   *   *   *

As we returned home, there was still no call from the resort that had interviewed Sue before our departure. Eventually, she gave up leaving messages; we were learning the hard way how unprofessional and unreliable businesspeople can be here. At the beginning of August, I sat down with Santiago for our August monthly meeting. Santiago is pastor of our mother church, and I meet with him once a month to report on our progress and gain the benefit of his wisdom on all matters to do with church and life in Lanzarote.

As we reflected on the recent failure of the café, Sue's lack of work, and our consequently depleted financial resources, I mentioned to him that I was looking for ways to earn a bit more money. He immediately offered me a great opportunity. 'Why don't you go out and sell the water purification systems that José Enrique's company does?' José Enrique is the president of our denomination in the Canary Islands, a lovely man and quite an entrepreneur, as it turns out. He has the franchise for top quality water purification systems that turn our dodgy desalinated tap water into a personal spring of the finest, purest water you could ever hope to find anywhere.

Selling water: What could be simpler? 'You can sell to the English and Germans', Santiago enthusiastically suggested. 'It's easy. Nobody in their right mind drinks the tap water here. They all buy huge five-litre plastic bottles of mineral water, often delivered once a week, just like milk used to be back in England in years gone by. Otherwise it's a matter of carrying several heavy bottles home from the supermarket every week. Why not swap all that bother for the convenience of your own supply of pure water at the turn of the tap?'

And so it was that after two days' training I was ready to go out and earn a good living peddling the many benefits of these wonderful systems. That is, once I had the appropriate equipment, which would be available 'very soon'. A few weeks later I was the proud owner of a new set of gadgets: a conductivity meter to measure the amount of gunk dissolved in our water, and an electrolyte to bring it out of solution, turning a glass of clear inviting water into a revolting cocktail of black-and-green slime. Impressive or what!?

The water quality here in the south of the island is extraordinarily bad. The conductivity meter measures the number of particles of dissolved solids per million, of which healthy water contains fewer than 150. The 'drinking water' coming out of my tap contained three and a half times that. My astonishment and alarm grew further when I measured the water coming out of our organic carbon filter; there were even more solids than in the unfiltered water! The main thing the carbon seemed to take out was the chlorine, which in itself was no bad thing; according to a Spanish newspaper article that formed part of our presentation, chlorine kills an incredible sixty thousand people a year in Spain through bladder cancer.

As I've already said, everybody knows the tap water is poor quality. What they don't realise, however, is that the mineral water they are purchasing is often not much better. On top of that, it takes up a lot of room in the kitchen. Finally there's the terrific environmental damage caused by the disposal of all that plastic. Apparently one million seabirds die every year, choked by the evil stuff.

There is just one catch when it comes to selling: you have to first convince the good people of Lanzarote that they really would like a visit from your trustworthy self! Of course, the first port of call for all new salesmen is inevitably friends and family. Having no family here, that leaves friends. Our closest friends being very supportive, they kindly agreed to be our guinea pigs.

Naturally the first question they all asked, to test our sincerity was,

'Have you got one?' At this stage the answer was, 'Not yet'. The thing was that, with the hesitation over investing five hundred euros myself and the slowness of the company in fitting the system, the 'week' from beginning the sales venture to becoming the proud owners of our own system turned into a month, two months, and finally *five* months!

Meanwhile, our first customers, a lovely older couple and great supporters of ours in the church, received the installation of one fine model, along with the bonus of one fine mess of a flood one morning soon after! As if that wasn't enough, when our own system was finally fitted some while later, blow me down if the same thing didn't happen again! Finally, having exchanged a series of emails with the marketing manager, we had a wonderful new system installed at a knock-down price. All's well that ends well!

Nevertheless, all my further efforts to sell failed completely. I even gave up a whole weekend to attend a huge sales fair, where I was assured I would be guaranteed to sell. While my Canarian colleagues captured customers, I didn't get even one. I felt the worst I had since our move.

Although it was my birthday on the Sunday, sharing a lovely cake with my friends on the stand was a poor consolation! I felt really bad about missing the church service to do secular work. My sense of guilt was intensified when I received a call from Gerie, who was running the church service and struggling to get the projection equipment working.

To top it all, my only lead from the weekend campaign was a disaster commercially; I even managed to electrocute myself while using the electrodes to separate the solids from the water!

The failed attempt to turn my one lead into a sale had taken me to one of the remotest parts of the island, meaning a long, wasted journey. If that wasn't bad enough, my trip home nearly ended in disaster. I had already experienced the mencaces of 'local loco' and 'dozy tourist'. Now it was time to meet with the rarest of the dangerous beasts that habitually roam these parts, and make driving such a hazardous occupation. Any of the three can appear in the driver's field of view at any moment, causing anything from mild alarm to potentially fatal obstruction.

I'm talking about the Canarian Podenco hunting dog. The evidence of hunting activity in progress is easy to spot as one drives through the dark volcanic rocky parts of the landscape—4x4s parked just off the road with cages on the back. They have pulled over to allow the beasts to jump down and pursue whatever prey may emerge from a gap between the rocks, which doubles as the backdoor to a local unsuspecting rabbit and his or her many relations.

Of course, while the hounds are busy chasing the quarry, there is no conflict with the average road user. Problems only arise on the sad occasions when, having finished a fruitless pursuit, they find themselves in the middle of nowhere and abandoned by their owner. The latter has already returned home triumphantly clutching several braces of long, fat *conejos*. The pathetic *perros*, now stranded far from home without a lift in the back of one of those otherwise ubiquitous trucks, start to wander the countryside.

I was driving home along the fast, straight stretch of road that brings me from the pretty town of Yaiza down to the coast where I live. This is the 'new road'. When the time came to improve this route a couple of years previous to our arrival, the old one, which is rather narrower and clings scenically to the meandering coastline, was left untouched. The new road was built just inland from the old one along a straighter line. Hence the two converge and diverge at various points, creating an unnerving phenomenon when it comes to considering whether to pass one of the more relaxed drivers. Is that lorry hurtling toward me on my road or the other one? An error of judgment would be fatal, so no degree of uncertainty can be tolerated in these circumstances!

Now, there is a feature of Spanish traffic law that was politely pointed out to me by a gentleman of the Guardia on one occasion. It is forbidden to overtake when the traffic is 'pegado', literally 'stuck together', or in other words, if there's not enough room between vehicles to allow one to pass them one at a time and pull in easily. The logic of this rule is clear, especially when people are frequently given to pulling out blindly without checking their rear view.

On the afternoon in question, I came up behind just such a slow moving column of tourists. They were most definitely 'pegado', as they lumbered along like some articulated metal monster, restricting me to 70 per cent of my preferred velocity. The temptation to violate the prohibition and whizz past the whole lot was fierce. Thankfully, I chose to 'peg' myself to the back of the caravan and join the slow procession. After all, we were within a few minutes' drive of the large roundabout that marks the edge of my hometown, even at that slow pace; so the delay would not be overwhelming.

Suddenly the car in front of me swerved away from the kerb. As is the case with this type of incident, the scene before me played out in slow motion. The looping trajectory of the vehicle revealed the parallel and opposite path of a nonchalant hunting dog, which mounted the carriageway from the scrubby embankment, quickly sensed that the monster of which I formed one segment was significantly higher up the food chain and trotted down off the roadway without even blinking!

That was it! Any remaining gap in my resolve to quit the water job was now firmly sealed. It was clearly a dangerous occupation, and I was obviously not cut out to be a salesman. I returned to what I had been doing previously, working with the language.

On the brighter side, it was a relief and an encouragement to see Paul gain some stable employment at last. Despite the gloomy economic outlook, with the tourist trade taking a distinct downturn, he had managed to get a job with a contract at one of the more successful restaurants in Puerto del Carmen.

*　　*　　*　　*　　*

Our September pastors' gathering turned out to be most memorable. I must have been feeling more comfortable with my colleagues despite the language barrier because I was in a daring mood. The only problem is that such a disposition makes one vulnerable to embarrassing mistakes where the language is concerned. My most shocking mistake had been a few years earlier. The Spanish word *joder* is pronounced 'ho dare'. Its similarity in sound to the English expression 'Oh dear' along with the similar ideas of mild surprise and consternation it evidently carried led me to believe the two were equivalent. I only suspected my error when I used it in an email to a friend, and her response was, 'Why are you so angry?' Turning to the dictionary, I was dismayed to find the true meaning. This was the Spanish 'F word'. Oh dear indeed!

On this occasion, we were meeting in the northern village of Tinajo, where the church community had been busy renovating the old school, which had fallen into disuse, and had now been lent to them by the town council. When it came to lunchtime an extraordinary dish called *tamal* appeared: huge mounds of food enveloped in silver foil to keep it piping hot.

As I carefully folded back the silver leaves to reveal another layer, this time thick, dark-green, and glistening with moisture. On peeling back this second leaf, there appeared a deliciously steaming stew of marinated meats, eggs, and vegetables. I learned later that this Colombian speciality is a traditional Christmas dish prepared painstakingly in time for midnight on Christmas Eve, and the large green leaves are those of the banana plant.

Naturally, our hosts were keen to learn my opinion of the meal they had presented with such aplomb. They announced the name of the dish, '*es tamal*' ('it's tamal'). I immediately felt this was an opportunity for me to have a bit of fun with the language. Their announcement sounded the same as the phrase '*está mal*', meaning 'it's bad'. I piped up, 'You said it was bad; I don't think it's bad!'

After a bit of confusion, they got the joke. Just as satisfying as the food was my contentment, seasoned with a sense of relief, having been able to play with the words in Spanish. It was only a small phrase, and I'd had to explain my humour; but that didn't stop me from congratulating myself!

A similar humorous incident occurred the following week. The local chemist that I frequented once a month with my regular prescriptions had been due to move premises to the centre of town a couple of months previously. For something to say, I attempted to remark, 'So you're still here'. My '*Seguís aquí*' was misheard. The friendly girl behind the counter thought I said, '*¿Se guisa aquí?*', which translated means 'Do you cook here?' A rather bizarre question even for a quirky foreigner like myself!

*   *   *   *   *

That year, winter had arrived early in the United Kingdom and even down here. Back there it was snowing at the end of October. Here we'd had rain, not much by English standards, but rain nevertheless. At night, the odd short shower had been beating an unfamiliar rhythm on the flat roof of our bedroom, and at times we'd had to use the windscreen wipers when driving.

All this winteriness had arrived on a blast of cold air emanating from the polar regions. The importance of this when meeting visitors at the airport is that the strong northerly wind blowing at over one hundred miles an hour in the upper atmosphere can bring forward landing times by up to forty minutes. Therefore, in order to avoid them having to wait for us to pick them up, which I find most tedious and unwelcoming after a long day travelling, we carefully took the wind into account and presented ourselves early at Arrivals. As you can probably guess, although they had spent thirty five minutes less time in the air than scheduled, delays at both ends added up to an hour's wait for us. Never mind, all this was quickly forgotten at the joy of being reunited with my lovely sister and her fine husband.

Poor Nicky had just undergone some painful surgery on her knee, which had been damaged from years of accompanying her beloved on his athletic outings. Thankfully for her, she could still cycle, so bikes were duly hired and they heroically rolled up the long sloping roads under the hot autumn sun as far as Fire Mountain. 'I remember every sweaty moment as I slogged along behind Tony!' Nicky recounts with feeling.

As they pulled up panting at the top, they were greeted with a round of admiring applause from the incredulous crowd of tourists, recently arrived in their hire cars and coaches.

The odd shower wasn't enough to dampen Nicky and Tony's spirits.

On our day off, we took them to see Omar Sharif's former house, Lagomar.

As we sat overlooking the coast from the heights of Nazaret and tucked into our picnic lunch, Nicky enthused about the island. 'I just love this place. Every time we come, I surprise myself at the wow factor it gives me'.

Sue responded, 'It's very nice for us to hear comments like that, because it helps us to appreciate it as well'.

Nicky continued. 'Then I think, would I feel the same if I lived and worked here? And the answer is, I would, because I do at home in the same way. We can do our local usual training ride on the tandem, which takes us over some lovely areas of countryside. And every time we come over the same stretches of road, and we look to our right and our left, over these beautiful views, I take the same big breath and gaze and drink it in'.

Sue agreed. 'Yes, I have places like that, which I particularly love. But it's still nice when people come and enthuse, because it makes us look at the island through different eyes. And that helps us to appreciate it again, afresh really'.

*   *   *   *   *

As the year came to an end and I was reflecting on our life on the island, I realised a fundamental truth that had been slowly emerging from my subconscious, which I'd been puzzling since our arrival. Grant's assertion that we shouldn't believe a thing he said, paradoxical as it may sound, had turned out to be thoroughly true and reliable. For one thing, we live on a small island, among an even smaller community of British expats, the vast majority of whom don't understand the language and, consequently, what's going on around them. A good example had been the unfounded rumours about sudden climate change in general and hurricanes in particular.

Another aspect of life that lends itself to the communication of untruth is the whole area of paperwork and bureaucratic procedures that Grant worked with, and which I had now experienced first-hand. Examples of the about-turns and abrupt changes in bureaucratic procedures are as legion as they are legendary. I was discussing the whole issue one balmy evening as we were once again enjoying David and Liz's warm hospitality in the congenial company of old friends of theirs from England, who had worked in local government back in the Sixties. They were depressingly familiar with the sorry scenario, where each department is like a silo; all these servants of the state know is their own narrowly focused sphere of work, and for all they care, the world outside might as well not exist.

After the NIF, the next most important document to obtain here is the *residencia*. This proof of residency is the key to half-price fights within Spanish territory and essential for getting access to the health service. At eleven o'clock one sunny December morning, Sue and I were guiding some of our very first customers through the idiosyncrasies of the tortuous procedure, and she was sitting in the police station with them, when suddenly one of the clerks sprang to their feet and announced agitatedly that the fee had just gone up by ten eurocents. He then proceeded to gesticulate wildly, turning away the thirty or so people who had been queuing for an hour or more and instructing them to return once they'd paid the extra fee.

Admittedly it is difficult to appreciate why that should be such a dramatic event, until the intricate mechanics of the means of expediting said payment are laid bare. First of all, the payment is not made in the office; it can be made at any one of a number of banks. However, all the banks within walking distance restrict the hours between which payment of this nature can be made. Notably, no payment is ever accepted after eleven o'clock. The implication, then, is that everybody waiting to be served had to leave post-haste, jump into a vehicle, and drive to the closest bank that was not within walking distance to pay their ten eurocents.

So Grant was right. Nobody should ever believe anything anybody ever tells you about Lanzarote. Having said that, of course my account is as true as my poor old memory will allow; I have just changed a few details to protect the innocent and not so innocent. Like the *Starship Enterprise*, the voyage we set out on three years ago has led to the exploration of a strange new world, and I have tried to communicate faithfully the impressions that this experience has left upon me.

The New Year found us like deer in the headlights of approaching bankruptcy. We had heard how people get stranded in this part of the world, with no means to pay their ticket home even; but we just couldn't believe that would happen to us.

We reflected with some perplexity on how we'd got into this mess. Sue had been promised so much work. To our great disappointment and consternation, all those promises failed dismally. The villa management business decided to do its own bookkeeping and the café ran at a loss for the short time it was open, so the only income Sue was able to derive from it was sparse. The wedding company employed her services for one day, declared their full satisfaction with her efforts, and repeatedly told her she could start 'next week' over a period of several months.

But the most extraordinary business had been the silence following Sue's interview the day before we departed on our summer holidays. False promises seem to be a common feature of recruitment or, rather, non-recruitment in Lanzarote. I am still at a loss to explain it. Perhaps I will have worked it out by the time I write my next book; that is, if we survive long enough here.

The fact is that with Sue out of work and our credit card debt consequently mounting, nothing short of a miracle would do. I summed up our feelings as we made on our last visit to the spa.

'Estamos tristes' ('we're sad'), I volunteered to the girl on the desk.

'Why?' she asked.

I explained that our year's membership was about to run out and there was no way we could afford to renew for another twelve months.

'But we're doing a very good offer on renewals', she rejoined. 'You get a 50 per cent discount'.

'That's very impressive', I responded, 'but our lack of money is even more so!'

It was looking like there would be no more sandwiches in the sun for us. Nonetheless, it had been an enjoyable adventure trying to settle into such a different country. If we had to return to England, then we may be financially drained, but the experience had been enriching in other ways that money cannot buy!

And yet things were going so well with the church. We couldn't believe it was time to move on and leave the rocky little island we now called home. We had even just achieved our biggest attendance in the three years. The record congregation of fifty was set in quite an extraordinary manner, not surprisingly given our experience of life on the quirky Canary Island. I had my head down trying to expel the latest gremlins from the church's cantankerous sound system when I became aware of a bit of a kerfuffle at the door. I looked up to see Paul and Ray hurriedly setting out two more rows of chairs at the back of the hall. Behind them was standing a crowd of tall burly blond men, which turned out to be the Faroe Islands soccer team!

As we began to sing, their presence was felt even more as their voices swelled in a powerful rich harmony, reminiscent of the legendary Treorchy Male Choir from Wales. It wasn't long after that the same group of men overtook the Welsh soccer team in the FIFA rankings.

But this occasion wasn't about international competition. On the contrary, as we gathered together, British, Africans, and Scandinavians, for me it was like a foretaste of heaven, with people from every tribe and tongue joining together in worship of the God who made us all from every nation and redeemed all.

CHAPTER 11

House for Sale: One Careful Owner

As THE DEBTS MOUNTED, our faith that it was indeed Almighty God who had sent us to Lanzarote was being fiercely tested. It was time once again to experience that strange mixture of nervous anxiety on one level and calm assurance on another. I was feeling much as I had done halfway through my theology course, waiting for divine intervention and quaking, yet knowing in my spirit it soon would come.

Or was I simply in denial? I really wasn't sure; it is such an effective mechanism for defence. The important thing was that I managed to put the threatening disaster out of my mind.

And that time there appeared, rather like the biblical star of Bethlehem, an extraordinary sight. It was an advertisement in the e-zine *Gazette Live* for an office job that might suit Sue.

On the face of it, the position was far from ideal, including as it did a bottom of the scale clerical salary, a thirty-five-minute drive to Matagorda, next to the airport, and the requirement of fluent Spanish. Sue submitted her CV without a lot of conviction. Nevertheless, she soon found herself attending her first interview.

Although Sue had been working away with a grim determination to improve her Spanish language skills, there's no way she would have described herself as fluent. So when it came to the Spanish part of the interview, she thought, *I've got nothing to lose; go for it!* Her interviewer, a personable lady in her thirties who appeared to be a partner in the firm, asked Sue about the book she was currently reading.

In a couple of days, Sue had been called back for a second interview. The task set was simple; while Joanna went out, Sue was to run the office for the morning!

'I could make a real mess of this', she mused in her bewilderment.

Of course, her resourcefulness and experience quickly came into play, as she dealt professionally with a stream of inquiries for holiday lettings and met competently every other challenge that came her way.

The very next day, Sue got the call she'd been waiting for. Only it wasn't a job offer, but a request to attend a third interview! This time she had to role-play showing an apartment to Brian, the boss.

'That was excellent!' Brian concluded.

Sue was incredulous. She could hardly believe it. Nevertheless, her potential boss had appeared completely sincere in his praise.

'We'll let you know by the end of the week, one way or another'.

Apart from needing the job to survive financially, the idea of taking the position had now grown on Sue. She had hit it off with Joanna and Brian, enjoyed her surprise morning's work, and been genuinely flattered by Brian's comments.

Friday came … and went. No call. We spent a tense weekend,

looking continually at Sue's phone for missed calls. Still nothing. It was like our French holiday all over again.

Why do these people always spoil our holidays and weekends? I thought, along with some less charitable sentiments.

I tried to keep Sue's spirits up. 'There must be a good reason they've not called yet. And anyway, as long as they don't call to say no, there's always hope'.

Monday morning at nine o'clock, Sue's phone rang. It was Joanna. 'Congratulations!'

The rest of the call was immaterial; our bacon had been saved!

We saw the hand of God in this quite clearly. He had stretched our faith, and hopefully it had grown in the process.

And so we were able to continue to live out our dreams, very conscious that, as Des'ree sang in her classic 1998 hit 'Life', 'Sometimes living out your dreams ain't as easy as it seems!'

That's life.